BHARATA NĀṬYAM
IN
CULTURAL PERSPECTIVE

Frontispiece: Alarmel Valli in *nrtta* pose. Photo: Thomas Foley.

BHARATA NĀṬYAM
IN
CULTURAL PERSPECTIVE

edited by

George Kliger

MANOHAR
AMERICAN INSTITUTE OF INDIAN STUDIES
NEW DELHI
1993

SSEA

ISBN 81-7304-034-6

First Published 1993

Published by Ajay Kumar Jain, Manohar Publishers & Distributors
2/6 Ansari Road, Daryaganj, New Delhi - 110 002 for
American Institute of Indian Studies,
D-31, Defence Colony, New Delhi - 110 024
and printed at Rajkamal Electric Press
B 35/9, G.T. Karnal Road Industrial Area
New Delhi - 110 003.

Contents

Illustrations

Frontispiece: Alarmel Valli in *nṛtta* pose. Photo: Thomas Foley.

Line Drawings (pages 70-80)
(All line drawings are by Suzanna Stough.)

Colorplates (following page 90)

Black and White Plates (following page 136)

Preface

Chapters II-VI of this volume are revised versions of five lectures, delivered in September 1984, three at the Minneapolis Institute of Arts and two at the University of Minnesota. Chapter I was written specially for this volume. The lectures were given in conjunction with the two-week residency of the renowned performing artist Padma Śrī * Alarmel Valli, foremost contemporary exponent of the Pandanallur style of Bharata Nāṭyam -- one of the major classical dance forms of India. The purpose of the lectures was to complement the activities and events of her residency; they included classes in the dance technique and music of Bharata Nāṭyam, lecture/demonstrations, choreography workshops, and dance recitals by Valli and accompanying musicians. We were all inspired by her magnificent performances and resolved to produce a volume which will contribute to an interdisciplinary understanding of a great living art form -- its intrinsic character as well as its historical, social and cultural context. Contributing scholars come from a variety of disciplines, including philosophy and humanistic studies, dance ethnology, ethnomusicology, art history, and comparative history.

In Chapter I, I trace the history of classical dance in the Tamil region, as it was affected by the emergence and growth of the Bhakti movement of religious devotionalism; the institution of dance as a mode of temple worship performed by female dancers known as *devadāsīs;* and the vicissitudes of political history. I then discuss the

* In recognition of her outstanding art, the title of Padma Śrī was conferred on Valli in 1991.

political, social and cultural developments of recent times and their effect on the present status and character of the classical dance of Tamil Nadu -- now known as Bharata Nāṭyam. Finally, I indicate the sources of the theory, technique, style, and continuing development of Bharata Nāṭyam as currently practiced, describe its abstract and mimetic components, and conclude with a description of the typical sequence of items featured in contemporary Bharata Nāṭyam recitals.

In Chapter II, I discuss what has become the foundation of Indian aesthetics, i.e., the theory of *rasa*, as well as a number of other concepts initially formulated in Bharata's *Nāṭyaśāstra* and developed further in subsequent literature on dramaturgy, dance, and poetics. I then analyze the mimetic/expressive (*nṛtya, abhinaya*) component of Bharata Nāṭyam, the influence of Bhakti and of royal patronage on its content, and explore the ways in which the concepts and principles referred to above are exemplified in it. Finally, I call attention to the recent trend toward popularization among teachers and performers of Bharata Nāṭyam.

In Chapter III, Professor Van Zile examines two basic units of pure (abstract) dance movement (*aḍavus*) and their variants, frequently employed in Bharata Nāṭyam, and derives from them a number of formal characteristics, such as the frontal, planar, and angular qualities, which define the pure dance style of Bharata Nāṭyam as we know it today.

In Chapter IV, Professor Kagan analyzes the musical form and content of each item in a typical Bharata Nāṭyam recital. His account emphasizes religious devotionalism (*bhakti*) as the main source of inspiration for the music of Bharata Nāṭyam. In the course of his analysis he is concerned to demonstrate the following points: music and song composed or adapted for dance are properly regarded as distinctive genres, governed by their function of constituting the musical dimension of dance, and as such they operate under constraints absent in pure music; however, their special role also provides distinctive opportunities for artistic creativity.

In Chapter V, Professor Rabe explores the parallels and mutual "mirrorings" of dance and sculpture in India, focusing on examples in Tamil Nadu. He explains these interrelations as deriving from (1) the fact that both art forms communicate almost exclusively through the human figure; (2) a shared aesthetic emphasis -- based on Purāṇic and *śāstraic* authority -- on "poetic" modes of stylizing conventions and suggestion, rather than "prosaic" or realistic representation; (3) a shared aesthetic tradition of emphasizing the realization of pre-existing paradigms or compositions in the arts, rather than inventiveness or originality; (4) a shared theological tradition of highlighting the immanent manifestations of the divine in the world in the form of dynamic activity; (5) the direct influence of sculpture on dance. In conclusion, Professor Rabe proposes that the window and the mirror are fitting metaphors for Hindu sculpture and dance, respectively.

Chapter VI by Professor Kopf is a historiographical account of four images of the *devadāsī* and her role in Indian society: (1) the *devadāsī* as temple priestess whose sexual practices ensure fertility in nature and society; (2) the *devadāsī* as sexual slave, exploited by priests, kings and wealthy patrons; (3) the *devadāsī* as divine courtesan, modelled on the *apsaras* of Hindu mythology, and representing the fusion of eroticism and mysticism characteristic of major trends in post-Gupta Hinduism such as Tantrism and the Vaiṣṇava Sahajiyā cult of Bengal; (4) the *devadāsī* as celestial dancer, claimed to have been originally chaste, but to have degenerated into concubinage and prostitution because of the vicissitudes of history.

Funding for the five original lectures was provided by the Minnesota Humanities Commission in cooperation with the National Endowment for the Humanities. The Humanities Department, University of Minnesota, provided funds to cover the cost of photography featuring Valli in various iconographic and dance poses. I am grateful to Jeanne Long, secretary of the Humanities Department, University of Minnesota, for her patient and diligent labors on the typescript.

George Kliger

Minneapolis, Minnesota

Contributors

Professor *ALAN L. KAGAN* teaches in the School of Music, University of Minnesota, Minneapolis, Minnesota.

Professor *GEORGE KLIGER* teaches in the Department of Humanities, University of Minnesota, Minneapolis, Minnesota.

Professor *DAVID KOPF* teaches in the Department of History, University of Minnesota, Minneapolis, Minnesota.

Professor *MICHAEL RABE* teaches in the Art Department, St. Xavier College, Chicago, Illinois.

Professor *JUDY VAN ZILE* teaches in the Music Department, University of Hawaii at Manoa, Honolulu, Hawaii.

Pronunciation

The following is a guide to Sanskrit pronunciation for the general reader.

Stress

Stress is placed on the last heavy syllable other than the last syllable of the word. If the word does not contain heavy syllables, stress should be placed as far back as possible, up to four syllables from the end. A syllable is heavy if it contains a long vowel (*ā*, *ī*, *ū*), a diphthong (*e*, *ai*, *o*, *au*), or a vowel followed by more than one consonant.

Vowels

a as *u* in b*u*t

ā as *a* in f*a*ther

i as *i* in f*i*t

ī as *i* in mar*i*ne

u as *u* in p*u*t

ū as *u* in r*u*le

ṛ (a vowel) as *ri* in *ri*d

e as *ei* in v*ei*n

ai as *ai* in *ai*sle

o as *o* in s*o*

au as *ou* in h*ou*nd

y as *y* in *y*es

Consonants

m, *ṅ* as *n* in li*n*k

g as *g* in *g*et

c as *ch* in *ch*art

j as *j* in *j*ust

ñ as *ñ* in se*ñ*or

ś, *ṣ* as *sh* in *sh*arp

s as *s* in *s*un

Aspirated Consonants

kh as *kh* in pac*k-h*orse

gh as *gh* in do*gh*ouse

th as *th* in ho*th*ouse

dh as *dh* in ma*dh*ouse

ph as *ph* in u*ph*ill

bh as *bh* in clu*bh*ouse

A distinction between retroflex consonants (formed with the tongue curled backward against the palate) *ṭ*, *ṭh*, *ḍ*, *ḍh*, *ṇ*, and dental consonants (formed with the tip of the tongue against or near the upper front teeth) *t*, *th*, *d*, *dh*, *n*, is recognized in Sanskrit but not in English.

I

Bharata Nāṭyam: History, Cultural Heritage and Current Practice

George Kliger

Bharata Nāṭyam as currently practiced is one of the major classical dance forms in existence. Its rich repertory of poetical texts; its highly developed vocabulary of expressive gestures; its intricate syntax of pure dance patterns; its music, displaying a wealth of complex rhythms and melodies; its sumptuous costumes--all make it one of the most sophisticated dance traditions in the world. When performed by an accomplished dancer and fine musicians it affords aesthetic experience of the highest order. It is rapidly becoming known and appreciated all over the world, as indeed it deserves to be.

I

Although the present form of Bharata Nāṭyam is of relatively recent origin, it represents a continuous, if occasionally eclipsed, tradition traceable to the distant past. It may indeed be the remote descendant of the well-known copper figurine of what appears to be a young female dancer from Mohenjo Daro (ca. 2300-1750 B.C.).[1] The figurine might even represent a member of a class of dancers who served in temples in the centers of Harappā Culture, in which case there may be a historical link between these ancient temple dancers and the later institution of the *devadāsī* which flourished in India in the Middle Ages. All this, however, is highly speculative, since there exits at present no independent evidence to support these conjectures.

In historical times there is abundant evidence of the importance of dance as a performing art in Indian culture generally, and specifically in Tamil society where Bharata Nāṭyam originated and evolved. Surviving texts of the golden age of Tamil literature and poetry known as the Śangam Age (early centuries A.D.) such as the *Tolkāppiyam*, as well as the later *Śilappadikāram* (ca. 600 A.D.),[2] testify to a variety of dance traditions which flourished in these times. The latter work is of particular importance for our theme, since one of its main characters, the courtesan Mādhavi, is a highly accomplished dancer. The *Śilappadikāram* is a mine of information on ancient Tamil culture and society, in which the arts of music and dance were highly developed and played a major role.[3]

When the dynasties of the Pallavas of Kāñcī and the Pāṇḍyas of Madurai dominated the Tamil region (sixth through ninth centuries A.D.), a great transformation in religious consciousness occurred, known as the Bhakti movement. It was an upsurge of fervent religious devotionalism centered on a personal deity--Viṣṇu or Śiva--which originated among the Tamils and eventually spread to the entire Indian subcontinent. Each sect had its own saints and developed its own characteristic mode of worship. However, they shared a common spirit of passionate religious devotion and a set of attitudes and values which have continued to play a vital role in Indian culture to this day.

In his highly perceptive study of the early Bhakti movement and its Tamil origins,[4] A.K. Ramunujan notes, among others, the following salient characteristics of *bhakti*: (1) the emphasis on the god's personal, immanent presence in the world and his accessibility to the *bhakta* (devotee); (2) the desire to participate in, be possessed by, even to incarnate the deity one worships; (3) the urge to "dance and sing one's god," depict him in poetry, painting, and sculpture, and build shrines to him; (4) the tendency to express one's devotion in popular, vernacular "mother tongues" in preference to the formal, hieratic language of Sanskrit accessible only to the few; (5) experiencing one's relation to god as that of a lover, on the analogy to human sexual passion--the predominant mood here being that of the lover's longing for union with the beloved, technically known as *viraha bhakti*, rather than the bliss of union. As Ramanujan makes clear, *bhakti* appealed to all strata of society, regardless of caste or gender. Vaiṣṇavite and Śaivite *bhakti* saints known as Āḻvārs and Nāyaṉārs, respectively, included in their ranks women and untouchables, in sharp contrast to the religious tradition of the "twice born" based on the Vedas, from which untouchables, śūdras and, in large measure, women had been rigorously excluded.

The Bhakti movement expressed itself in a multitude of ways in Tamil culture and society. Nāyaṉārs and Āḻvārs wandered throughout the Tamil country singing and reciting devotional songs and poems which they themselves had composed. They had a tremendous appeal to simple folk, but in many instances also converted monks and local rulers from Buddhism or Jainism (both were popular at the time) to Śaivism or Vaiṣṇavism. Indeed, so powerful was the Bhakti movement that it eclipsed and eventually succeeded in almost totally eliminating Buddhism and Jainism in South India.[5] Concomitant with these events, there occurred a veritable explosion of temple building which, beginning under the Pallavas, accelerated and reached its zenith under the Cōḻas of Tanjore (ninth to thirteenth century A.D.). Rock-cut temples were succeeded by structural temples. The building and embellishment of temples and the evolution of temple worship attracted many types of creative talent in architecture, sculpture, painting, poetry, music, and dance. Magnificent structures with soaring towers proliferated, housing icons of deities and saints cast in bronze; and adorned with depictions of mythological events, deities, celestial musicians and dancers, sages, and heroes, exquisitely carved in stone on pillars, walls, and towers (see Chapter V, Plates 1,3,5,6,7,8). Devotional poetry and songs composed by *bhakti* saints were recited, sung, and interpreted in the medium of expressive dance, as regular parts of temple service. The creative energies of the people were channeled into multifarious expressions of religious devotion.[6]

Kings of neighboring territories vied with each other in commissioning the building of splendid temples and providing for their maintenance and beautification by grants of tax-exempt land and treasure. Gifts to temples for upkeep, renovation, adornment, maintenance of staff, etc., were well-nigh universal, each worshipper contributing according to his/her means. As a consequence, the Hindu temple became, in time, the wealthiest and most powerful social, economic, and cultural institution outside of the royal court-- as well as serving in its capacity as a center of religious worship. In the words of one scholar "[The medieval Hindu temple] acted [among other things] as landholder, employer, consumer of goods and services, bank, school, museum, hospital, and theatre."[7]

The institution of the *devadāsī* evolved in the context of temple ritual. *Devadāsī* means, literally, "female slave (or servant) of God." *Devadāsīs* were women who, at an early age, were married and thus dedicated to the god of a particular temple. They sang and danced daily, at specified times, before the image of the deity they were serving--in the temple or at religious festivals when the image was carried in procession through the streets of city, town, or village. They also performed at royal courts and at family functions, such as weddings, in the homes of wealthy patrons. In these latter roles they were known as *rājadāsīs* and *alaṃkāradāsīs*, respectively. The earliest epigraphical evidence of the existence of the *devadāsī* institution in India is an inscription of the second century B.C. in a cave at Ramgarh, in Central India. In Tamil Nadu, the earliest definite evidence of the existence of the *devadāsī* institution is found in a class of sacred texts called Āgamas, most of which were probably composed during the eighth and ninth centuries A.D. They prescribe, among other things, modes of worship in the temple, including the consecration of female dancers to certain deities. There is ample epigraphical evidence of the growth and efflorescence of the *devadāsī* institution during the period of Cōḻa dominance. For example, we learn from an inscription that the magnificent Bṛhadīśvara temple of Tanjore (ca.1000 A.D.) employed 400 *devadāsīs*!

By Cōḻa times, the *devadāsīs* had crystallized into a distinct caste. Typically, although by no means invariably, the biological or adopted daughters of *devadāsīs* were trained in music and dance from an early age, and followed their mothers' occupation of temple service. The sons of *devadāsīs* were trained from boyhood to become *naṭṭuvanars*--teachers, directors and musical accompanists of dance. It was the *devadāsīs* and *naṭṭuvanars*, sponsored, protected and endowed with generous grants by kings, queens, nobles and wealthy merchants, who developed the techniques and styles of dance to a high degree of artistic perfection, and transmitted what they had developed from generation to generation, down the centuries.[8]

The period of Cōḻa dominance was followed by the re-emergence of the Pāṇḍyas of Madurai, who by the mid-thirteenth century established themselves as the central dynastic power in the Tamil region. In 1310 one of two contenders for succession to the Pāṇḍya throne appealed for military assistance to Malik Kafur, the Muslim invader from the North. Kafur indiscriminately sacked and plundered all cities and temples he encountered and returned with a vast booty to Delhi (where a sultanate had been established in 1206). A period of political upheavals ensued, during which a large part of the kingdom of Madurai became a province of the sultanate of Delhi. In 1334 the Sultan's provincial governor established an independent sultanate of Madurai, which lasted until 1370, when Kumāra Kampana, a prince of the Hindu kingdom of Vijayanagar (established in 1336) ousted the Madurai Sultan and consolidated the power of Vijayanagar in the South. The period of political strife and the

Muslim invasion and dominance from 1310 to 1370 had a disruptive effect on the cultivation and further development of the arts in the Tamil region. Temples were looted and destroyed; patronage of music and dance declined or stopped altogether; and performing artists, lacking customary means of support, were forced to fend for themselves. Some turned to other occupations, others departed for other regions of the subcontinent in search of employment. It is likely that, as a consequence, some techniques and styles of dance were lost forever.

With the establishment of Vijayanagar power in the South, patronage of the arts was resumed under the auspices of Hindu rulers. Epigraphical evidence and accounts by travelers indicate that music, dance and the *devadāsī* institution flourished throughout the empire. In 1565, Vijayanagar suffered a disastrous defeat in the battle of Talikota, when the combined armies of the Muslim sultanates of the Deccan routed the imperial army. Soon after, the empire disintegrated. In Tamil Nadu a number of vassals of the empire, known as Nāyaks, declared their independence of the now weakened central authority and established autonomous kingdoms, the most important of which were those of Tanjore and Madurai.

The Nāyaks of both kingdoms were great patrons of the arts, and during their reign there was a rich and varied development of music and dance. Compositions of forms of dance music such as *alārippu*, *svarajati*, *padam*, *varṇam*, *jatisvaram*, *śabdam*, as well as forms of dance drama such as Yakṣagāna and Kuravañji, proliferated. The Tanjore Nāyak rulers were not only generous patrons of music and dance; some of them were themselves scholars, poets, musicologists, connoisseurs of dance and composers of dance music and dance dramas. Vijayarāghava Nāyak (1633-1673), for example, was the patron of one of the greatest composers of *padams*, Kṣetrajña, but was also a composer in his own right, as was his illustrious predecessor Raghunātha Nāyak (1600-1634). Throughout the period of Nāyak rule *devadāsīs* prospered and were held in high regard.

Music, dance, and the *devadāsī* institution continued to prosper when the rule of Tanjore passed from the Nāyaks to the Maratha dynasty founded by Ekoji I in 1676. As had been the case with the Nāyak rulers, the Marathas were patrons, connoisseurs, and contributors to the arts of music and dance. It was during the reign of the Maratha *rājā* Tulaja II (1763-1787) that the three greatest composers of Carnatic music--Tyāgarāja, Muthuswāmi Dīkṣitar, and Śyāmā Śāstrī--flourished. The development of classical dance and dance music in Tamil Nadu culminated in the work of four brothers--the sons of the *naṭṭuvanar* Subbaraya--Ponniah, Chinniah, Vaḍivelu, and Śivanandam, known as the Tanjore Quartette. They worked under the patronage of Serfoji II (1798-1832), himself a poet and composer of dance music. The Tanjore Quartette perfected and codified the technique of Bharata Nāṭyam and established its typical repertoire of dance items as we know them today.

The death of Śivaji II in 1855 brought to an end Maratha rule in Tamil Nadu, and with it the royal patronage that had sustained many illustrious figures in the fields of scholarship, literture, poetry, music and dance. Under British rule the status and fortunes of the *devadāsīs* declined drastically. In many instances they were reduced to poverty and, not infrequently, resorted to prostitution. The dance of the *devadāsīs*, then called Sadir in its solo form, fell into disrepute. A number of persons holding influential positions in society formed a reform movement whose goal was the abolition of the *devadāsī* institution. They pointed to facts such as the widespread incidence of concubinage and prostitution among *devadāsīs*, and the occasional abduction of young girls for dedication to temple service. The indigenous reform movement received strong encouragement and support from the British government which, under the sway of Victorian morality, could not tolerate the existence of an institution whose members were performing religious functions in temples as well as engaging in dubious sexual practices. Bills prohibiting the dedication of girls to temple service were introduced in several South Indian states--first in Mysore in 1910, then in Travancore in 1930, and finally in the Madras Presidency (which, at the time, included the regions of Tamil Nadu and Andhra Pradesh) in 1947.

The *devadāsīs* had been the chief repositories of the techniques and styles of classical dance. With their decline the very existence of these dance traditions as living art forms was endangered. Fortunately, while the reform movement mentioned above was gathering momentum, there was simultaneously an awakening of interest in India's cultural traditions throughout the subcontinent. A number of influential persons--partly under the stimulus of Western artists such as the famous ballerina Anna Pavlova, who had become fascinated with Indian classical dance traditions--delved into India's rich heritage of music and dance.

Members of respectable brahmin families such as E. Krishna Iyer and, somewhat later, Rukmini Devi, dedicated themselves body and soul to rescuing the dance of the *devadāsīs* from the state of degradation and disrepute into which it had fallen. By the fourth decade of the twentieth century they succeeded in reestablishing it as one of India's most highly developed living art forms, a position which it shares with the two major styles of Indian classical music (the Southern or Carnatic and the Northern or Hindustani). In the process, the dance style which had been called Sadir was renamed Bharata Nāṭyam. In place of the temple or royal court of former times, Bharata Nāṭyam is now typically performed in a theater, concert hall or auditorium, while most of its leading exponents come from brahmin families, having thus replaced the *devadāsīs* of old.[9]

II

At present, the term "Bharata Nāṭyam" commonly refers to a solo dance form, usually performed by a woman. Its theory, technique, style and continuing development--for Bharata Nāṭyam is by no means mummified in its present state, but continues to evolve--derive from: (1) the living tradition as it has been preserved, developed further, and transmitted from generation to generation, from masters to pupils--the *guru-śiṣya paramparā* (literally, teacher-to-pupil line of transmission), each teacher cultivating and transmitting a specific style within the generic framework of Bharata Nāṭyam (these traditional stylistic lines of transmission are known as *Sampradāyas*); (2) the traditional technical treatises or *śāstras*, dealing with dance, of which the most important for Bharata Nāṭyam are the *Nāṭyaśāstra* attributed to the sage Bharata (dated no later than the sixth century A.D.),[10] the *Abhinayadarpaṇam* of Nandikeśvara (eleventh century A.D.?),[11] and the *Saṅgītaratnākara* of Śārṅgadeva (thirteenth century A.D.);[12] and (3) the sculptural depictions of basic movements of the dance known as *karaṇas*, as they were practiced at the time of the composition of the *Nāṭyaśāstra*. These movements, 108 in number, are said to have been invented by the god Śiva in his role as Naṭarāja or The Lord of Dance, and are described in Chapter IV of the *Nāṭyaśāstra* entitled *Tāṇḍavalakṣaṇam*. Each *karaṇa* is sculpturally depicted in a characteristic momentary "cross-section" carved in relief in vertical rows on projecting panels adorning the side walls of *gopurams*, or gateways surmounted by soaring towers, of the temple dedicated to Śiva Naṭarāja in Cidambaram, Tamil Nadu (fourteenth century A.D.--see, Chapter V, Plates 7 and 8). Among other Tamil temples featuring sculptural representations of *karaṇas* are the Bṛhadīśvara temple of Tanjore (ca. 1000 A.D.), and the Śāraṅgapāṇi temple of Kumbakoṇam. The Śāraṅgapāṇi carvings were probably executed toward the end of the twelfth century A.D. Both the *śāstras* and the sculptural depictions of *karaṇas* have been continuing sources of inspiration to choreographers of Bharata Nāṭyam to this day.[13]

There are two major elements in Bharata Nāṭyam: *nṛtta* or abstract, non-representational dance (see Chapter III, Frontispiece, and Colorplates I-IV), and *nṛtya* or representational-cum-expressive dance. The term *abhinaya* has come to be used as a near-synonym for *nṛtya* (see Chapter II and Colorplates V-VIII), but is also frequently used to refer to the means of expression employed by the dancer, such as voice, facial expression, hand gestures, etc. A third sense of *abhinaya* concerns the various ways in which a performer interprets a given text in terms of dance. The term *nāṭya* is often employed to refer to elements of plot, story line, or drama in dance, which can be viewed as subsumed in *nṛtya*.

Nṛtta, or abstract dance consists essentially of basic dance units known as *aḍavus*. Each *aḍavu* comprises a starting position, followed by a series of precise movements of head, neck, arms, hands, torso, legs and feet (see Chapter III). A sequence of *aḍavus* forms a *korvai*. Sequences of *aḍavus*, executed in intricate rhythmic patters, as the *naṭṭuvanar* recites the *sollukaṭṭu* (rhythmic syllables), are known as *jatis;* while sequences of *aḍavus* in the form of rhythmic flourishes, performed to the recitation of *sollukaṭṭu*, are called *tirmānams*.[14]

In an *abhinaya* item the dancer employs a language--i.e., a vocabulary and syntax--of denotative and expressive hand gestures, facial expressions, and body movements to interpret the text of a song. The rendition of the song itself and the instrumental music, executed by the vocalist and instrumentalists accompanying the dancer, make their own distinctive contributions to *abhinaya*.[15]

A typical contemporary Bharata Nāṭyam recital consists of the following items:

(1) *Alārippu*. An invocation addressed to the gods and the audience, executed as an abstract dance, essentially a warm-up for the artist and a first exhibit of pure dance in simple form.

(2) *Jatisvaram.* A rhythmically complex pure dance item, enabling the artist to exhibit mastery in precise coordination of footwork, musical notes and rhythmic beats.

(3) *Śabdam.* The first expressive dance item of the program. The dancer interprets through *abhinaya* the lines of a song in praise of a god or a royal patron.

(4) *Varṇam.* This is the centerpiece of the program. In it, the dancer typically impersonates the lovelorn *nāyikā,* or heroine longing for union with a divine or human lover. It is the most complex and longest in duration of all the items in the program--usually lasting from forty five minutes to an hour--and hence makes the greatest demands on the dancer's stamina and mastery of the art form. It consists of a series of alternating abstract and mimetic/expressive dance sequences based on a love song. The *varṇam* provides the artist with maximum opportunity to display both the rhythmically most complex sequences of pure dance *(nṛtta)* as well as the most varied and subtle interpretations of a poetic text in terms of mimetic/expressive dance (*abhinaya*).

The *varṇam* is followed by an intermission, after which the following items are usually performed:

(5) *Padam.* A leisurely *abhinaya* item based on a lyrical song expressive of the heroine's love for a god, symbolic of the human soul's desire for union with the divine. The mature dancer can elicit many nuances of feeling and mood in interpreting each line of the poetic text. In a full Bharata Nāṭyam recital several *padams* are usually presented.

(6) *Jāvali*. A romantic *abhinaya* piece, lighter than the *padam*, whose typical theme is worldly love.

(7) *Tillāna*. The concluding item of the concert, the *tillāna* is a pure dance item, featuring dazzling footwork executing a sequence of intricate rhythmic patterns in fast tempo, punctuated by sculpturesque poses. At its best the *tillāna* manifests to perfection the sheer visual beauty of abstract patterns of movement, and the clean, geometrical precision of form characteristic of the Bharata Nāṭyam style.[16]

Notes

1. Cf., e.g., Roy C. Craven, *A Concise History of Indian Art* (New York and Toronto: Oxford University Press, n.d.), p. 20 & Figure 11.

2. For an English translation see *The Anklet Story*: *Silappadhikaaram of Ilango Adigal*, rendered from the Tamil by Ka. Naa. Subramanyam (Delhi: Agam Prakashan, 1977).

3. Cf. Mohan Khokar, *Traditions of Indian Classical Dance*, 2nd rev. ed. (New Delhi: Clarion Books, 1984), pp. 74-75; K.A. Nilakanta Sastri, *The Culture and History of the Tamils* (Calcutta: Firma K.L. Mukhopadhyay, 1964), pp. 169-171.

4. A.K.Ramanujan, "Afterword," in *Hymns for the Drowning* (Princeton, New Jersey: Princeton University Press, 1981), pp. 103-169.

5. Cf. K.A. Nilakanta Sastri, *A History of South India*, 4th ed. (Madras: Oxford University Press, 1976), pp. 422-439.

6. Sastri, *The Culture and History of the Tamils*, pp. 154-169.

7. Devangana Desai, *Erotic Sculpture of India* (New Delhi: Tata McGraw-Hill Publishing Co., 1975), p. 159.

8. On the subject of the *devadāsī*, see Chapter VI. Also, cf. Desai, *Erotic Sculpture of India*, pp. 106-108, 161-64; A.L. Basham, *The Wonder That Was India* (New York: Grove Press, Inc., 1959), pp. 184-186; Khokar, *Traditions of Indian Classical Dance*, pp. 74-76. Frédérique Apffel Marglin's *Wives of the God-King: The Rituals of the Devadasis of Puri* (Delhi: Oxford University Press, 1985) is a scholarly, insightful study of the *devadāsī* institution in Orissa.

9. For an account of the evolution of Bharata Nāṭyam and its historical, social, and cultural context, from the perspective of a performing artist, see Lakshmi Viswanathan, *Bharatanatyam: The Tamil Heritage* (Madras: Sri Kala Chakra Trust, 1984). Also, cf. Sastri, *The Culture and History of the Tamils*, and Milton Singer, *When a Great Tradition Modernizes* (New York: Praeger Publishers, 1972), pp. 172-182.

10. Bharata Muni, *The Nāṭyaśāstra*, edited and translated by Manomohan Ghosh. Text: vol. I (Calcutta: Manisha Granthalaya Private Limited, 1967); vol. II (Calcutta, 1956). Translation: 2nd rev. ed., vol. I (Calcutta: Manisha Granthalaya Private Limited, 1967); vol. II (Calcutta: The Asiatic Society, 1961).

11. Nandikeśvara, *Abhinayadarpaṇam*, edited and translated by Manomohan Ghosh, 3rd ed. (Calcutta: Manisha Granthalaya Private Limited, 1975).

12. Śārṅgadeva, *Saṅgītaratnākara of Śārṅgadeva*, Sanskrit text and English translation by R.K. Shringy, vols. 1-2 (Delhi: Motilal Banarsidass, 1978-1989). While the *Nāṭyaśāstra* is the oldest of these, and regarded as the most authoritative by all the major classical dance traditions of India, contemporary Bharata Nāṭyam is more directly indebted to the latter two texts.

13. For a discussion of the interrelations of dance and sculpture in Tamil Nadu, see Kapila Vatsyayan, *Classical Indian Dance in Literature and the Arts* , 2nd ed. (New Delhi: Sangeet Natak Akademi, 1977), pp. 23-141, 316-319; and *Dance Sculpture in Sarangapani Temple* (Madras: Society for Archaeological, Historical and Epigraphical Research, 1982); Padma Subrahmanyam, *Bharata's Art: Then*

and Now (Bombay: Bhulabhai Memorial Institute, 1979), pp. 49-72; also, see Chapter V.

[14] Cf. Sunil Kothari, ed., *Bharata Natyam: Indian Classical Dance Art* (Bombay: Marg Publications, 1979), pp. 31-70.

[15] Ibid., pp. 17-22, 71-82.

[16] Ibid., pp. 83-92.

Bibliography

Adigal, Ilango, *The Anklet Story: Silappadhikaaram of Ilango Adigal*, rendered from the Tamil by Ka. Naa. Subramanyam (Delhi: Agam Prakashan, 1977).

Basham, A.L., *The Wonder That Was India* (New York: Grove Press, Inc., 1959).

Bharata Muni, *The Nāṭyaśāstra*, edited and translated by Manomohan Ghosh. Text: vol. I (Calcutta: Manisha Granthalaya Private Limited, 1967); vol. II (Calcutta, 1956). Translation: 2nd rev. ed., vol. I (Calcutta: Manisha Granthalaya Private Limited, 1967); vol. II (Calcutta: The Asiatic Society, 1961).

Craven, Roy C., *A Concise History of Indian Art* (New York and Toronto: Oxford University Press, n.d.).

Desai, Devangana, *Erotic Sculpture of India* (New Delhi: Tata McGraw-Hill Publishing Co., 1975).

Khokar, Mohan, *Traditions of Indian Classical Dance*, 2nd. rev. ed. (New Delhi: Clarion Books, 1984).

Kothari, Sunil, ed., *Bharata Natyam: Indian classical Dance Art* (Bombay: Marg Publications, 1979).

Marglin, Frédérique Apffel, *Wives of the God-King: The Rituals of the Devadasis of Puri* (Delhi: Oxford University Press, 1985).

Nandikeśvara, *Abhinayadarpaṇam*, edited and translated by Manomohan Ghosh, 3rd ed. (Calcutta: Manisha Granthalaya Private Limited, 1975).

Ramanujan, A.K., *Hymns for the Drowning* (Princeton, New Jersey: Princeton University Press, 1981).

Śārṅgadeva, *Saṅgītaratnākara of Śārṅgadeva*, Sanskrit text and English translation by R. K. Shringy, vols. 1-2 (Delhi: Motilal Banarsidass, 1978-1989).

Sastri, K.A. Nilakanta, *A History of South India*, 4th ed. (Madras: Oxford University Press, 1976).

Sastri, K.A. Nilakanta, *The Culture and History of the Tamils* (Calcutta: Firma K.L. Mukhopadhyay, 1964).

Singer, Milton, *When a Great Tradition Modernizes* (New York: Praeger Publishers, 1972).

Subrahmanyam, Padma, *Bharata's Art: Then and Now* (Bombay: Bhulabhai Memorial Institute, 1979).

Vatsyayan, Kapila, *Classical Indian Dance in Literature and the Arts*, 2nd ed. (New Delhi: Sangeet Natak Akademi, 1977).

Vatsyayan, Kapila, *Dance Sculpture in Sarangapani Temple* (Madras: Society for Archeological, Historical and Epigraphical Research, 1982).

Viswanathan, Lakshmi, *Bharatanatyam: The Tamil Heritage* (Madras: Sri Kala Chakra Trust, 1984).

II

Indian Aesthetics and Bharata Nāṭyam

George Kliger

From the point of view of subsequent developments of Indian aesthetics, literary theory and the performing arts, the most important extant text is undoubtedly the *Nāṭyaśāstra*,[1] attributed to the legendary sage Bharata. It is a compendium on theatre, music, and dance, regarded by scholars as a compilation, probably the product of several authors, dated not later than the sixth century A.D., but parts of which may be as old as the second century B.C.[2] This text contains comprehensive discussions of dramaturgy, dance, and music, which indicate that these arts had attained a high level of development at the time the work was completed. They show further that from very early times the three arts of acting, dance, and music have been essential ingredients of drama in ancient India. The *Nāṭyaśāstra* attributes the origin of drama to the creator god Brahmā who, having meditated on the four Vedas--the most sacred scriptures of Hinduism--took the verbal element from the *Ṛgveda*, song from the *Sāmaveda*, representation through acting from the *Yajurveda*, and sentiments (or moods) from the *Atharvaveda*, and created the *Nāṭyaveda*, i.e., the Veda concerned with the art of drama.[3] The ingredient of dance was then added to drama upon Śiva's recommendation[4]--Śiva being commonly regarded in Hindu tradition as the originator of the art of dance.

Chapters VI and VII of the *Nāṭyaśāstra* contain discussions of what ultimately came to be regarded in India as the most fundamental concepts of aesthetics, signified by the terms *rasa* and *bhāva*, commonly translated as "mood" and "emotion," respectively.[5] These concepts were taken up and developed mainly in the context of poetics.[6] They achieved their definitive formulation in the writings of two Kashmiri authors--Ānandavardhana, a ninth century literary critic and poet in his own right, and Abhinavagupta, an eleventh century philosopher, mystic, and connoisseur of the arts. These two authors developed the concepts of *bhāva* and *rasa* to a high degree of refinement.[7]

What, then, are *bhāvas* and *rasas* in the context of Indian aesthetics? The *Nāṭyaśāstra* distinguishes *sthāyi bhāvas,* or stable, dominant emotions, from *vyabhicāri bhāvas*, also often referred to as *sañcāri bhāvas*, or transitory emotional states. *Sthāyi bhāvas* are regarded as latent, stable dispositions--present in all of us, acquired as a result of experiences in numerous past lives--of responding in typical emotional ways to various life-situations. According to the *Nāṭyaśāstra* there are eight such dominant emotional states, or *sthāyi bhāvas*, namely, *rati*, sexual love; *hāsa*, laughter; *śoka*, sorrow; *krodha*, anger; *utsāha*, fortitude; *bhaya*, fear; *jugupsā*, disgust; and *vismaya*, astonishment.[8] Some subsequent authors added *nirveda*, world-weariness; others added *śama*, equanimity, as a ninth state.[9]

The *vyabhicāri bhāvas* or *sañcāri bhāvas* are transitory emotional states to which we are subject when in the grip of a dominant emotion. For example, when in love, we may experience longing, hope, anxiety, despondency, elation, etc., in rapid succession. These transitory states, then, are referred to as *vyabhicāri* or *sañcāri bhāvas*. Thirty-three transitory states are enumerated in the *Nāṭyaśāstra*.[10]

Emotional states are not objects of sense-perception as are physical objects or events in the physical world. They are subjective states of persons. Therefore they cannot be directly represented in some sensory artistic medium, as can physical objects or events. To be sure, one can *refer* to, e.g., the emotional state of love by using the word "love"; this, at best, communicates the idea of love, but does not evoke the emotion itself in the audience. Hence, in order to evoke in the audience an imaginative experience of an emotional state, the latter must be indirectly suggested by elements of a sensory medium which constitute adequate vehicles for conveying such a state.[11] In drama, emotional states are suggested or conveyed by what the *Nāṭyaśāstra* calls *vibhāvas*, observable causes or determinants of emotional states; *anubhāvas*, the overt expressions or manifest consequences of emotional states; and *sāttvika bhāvas*, the special class of involuntary overt expressions of emotional states, such as weeping, trembling, fainting, etc.[12]

To illustrate, the observable causes or determinants of a man's love for a woman are the woman's physical attributes, her personality traits as manifested in her behavior, and may also include the circumstances of their first encounter--e.g., meeting in a park in springtime. Overt consequences may include a change in the tone of his voice in her presence, smiling, etc.

The specific ways in which the observable causes and overt expressions of emotions are represented in drama and dance are referred to by the term *abhinaya*. Four kinds of *abhinaya* are enumerated in the *Nāṭyaśāstra*: *āṅgika abhinaya*, or gestures and movements of the body or any of its parts--including hand gestures and facial expressions; *vācika abhinaya*, or the use of speech and song; *sāttvika abhinaya,* or imitation of involuntary expressions of emotional states; and *āhārya abhinaya*, or dress and makeup.[13]

We now come to the most important idea of Indian aesthetics, namely, the concept of *rasa*.[14] *Rasa* literally means "flavor," "sap," "juice," or "essence." The term has been employed metaphorically in the context of aesthetics to indicate the joy, delight, or bliss of apprehending an emotional situation aesthetically. It is also used to refer to the emotional situation itself as the object of aesthetic experience. In real life we usually experience an emotional situation with some emotional involvement on our part. To be sure, when the situation in question affects others rather than ourselves we may be callous or indifferent. Thus in ordinary life our responses to emotional situations range from indifference to intense involvement. In Indian aesthetics this usual range of responses is labeled *laukika,* or ordinary. On the other hand, *rasa,* or the aesthetic experience of an emotional situation, is labeled *alaukika*, or extraordinary--the term is also sometimes translated as transcendental. There are two main features which distinguish *rasa* from an ordinary experience. First, in order to apprehend an emotional situation aesthetically we must neither identify with it nor attribute it to someone else with whom we may then sympathize. In other words, the emotion in question must be experienced by us as impersonal.[15] In modern parlance, we must have the attitude of aesthetic distance toward it. Second, we must find the emotional situation in question intrinsically interesting so that we becomes so absorbed in its contemplation as to forget ourselves in it--a state of consciousness which has been described in Western aesthetics as one of *intransitive attention*. When these two requirements are satisfied one experiences what has variously been described as a higher pleasure--higher, that is, than ordinary sensual pleasure--namely, pure unalloyed joy, or even bliss. The bliss of *rasa* has been compared by mystically oriented philosophers, such as Abhinavagupta, to *ānanda*, or the bliss attendant on the realization of ultimate truth. The experience of *rasa*, then, according to Abhinavagupta, gives us a foretaste of our ultimate goal in life, which is disentanglement from the snares of illusion and the consequent attainment of permanent bliss. *Rasa*, of course, differs from the latter in that it is evanescent in nature, since it lasts only as long as our absorption in a play, poem, musical performance, etc.[16]

In drama and dance *rasa* is suggested or evoked in the audience by *abhinaya* expressive of *sthāyi bhāvas* and *sañcāri bhāvas*, i.e., stable and transitory emotional states, by means of representing their *vibhāvas*, *anubhāvas* and *sāttvika bhāvas*--that is, their observable causes or determinants and their voluntary and involuntary overt expressions. The actor or dancer, however, must not simply imitate real-life emotional situations, for if that is done it is likely to evoke emotional involvement on the part of the audience rather than *rasa*--as is the case, for instance, when we watch a tear-jerker, as distinguished from a fine performance of a great tragedy. *Abhinaya* must be such as to trigger the appropriate *sthāyi bhāva* or latent permanent emotional disposition in each of us, and yet to enable us to objectify it, experience it as impersonal, and take delight in its contemplation.

Since *rasa* is the aesthetic contemplation of an emotional situation, there is a *rasa* corresponding to each *sthāyi bhāva*. Thus, using the term "mood" to designate *rasa* we have the following correspondences: *śṛṅgāra rasa*, the erotic mood, is evoked by a representation of, or corresponds to, love; *hāsya rasa*, the comic mood, corresponds to laughter; *karuṇa rasa*, the mood of pathos or compassion, corresponds to sorrow; *raudra rasa*, the furious mood, corresponds to anger; *vīra rasa*, the heroic mood, corresponds to fortitude; *bhayānaka rasa*, the mood of terror, corresponds to fear; *bībhatsa rasa*, the mood of loathing, corresponds to disgust; *adbhuta rasa*, the mood of wonder, corresponds to astonishment; and *śānta rasa*, the mood of tranquility, corresponds to world-weariness, according to some; equanimity, according to others.[17]

In the Indian tradition the concept of *rasa*, originally developed in the context of drama, dance, music, and poetry,[18] has come to be applied to all the arts. Anything which purports to be a work of art and which does not evoke or suggest a *rasa* is regarded as, at best, an inferior work of art or, at worst, as no art at all. While it is recognized that aesthetic delight can be experienced in contemplating an idea, an image, or a configuration of sound, visual form, color, and movement, the essence or soul of any work of art which lays claim to the name of art in a preeminent degree is held to be its evocation of *rasa*.

However, not everyone is capable of tasting *rasa*. The work of art or artistic performance does not automatically trigger an aesthetic experience in the viewer, listener, or reader. For such experience to occur, the development and cultivation of an aesthetic sensibility is required. Abhinavagupta's term for a person of aesthetic sensibility is *sahṛdaya*--literally, "one with heart." More commonly, he is known as a *rasika*, one capable of tasting *rasa*. Such capacity depends on the proper innate endowments, such as emotional sensitivity, and a knowledge of the pertinent conventions and techniques, as well as frequent exposure to the art form concerned.[19]

The *rasa* tradition in Indian aesthetics has profoundly affected the actual practice of the arts in India. As applied to dance, it accounts for the fact that *abhinaya*--which, with the support of music and lyrics, is the primary conveyer of *rasa* in this performing art--is a dominant element in all major classical dance traditions of India.[20] There is some variation, however, among the different traditions as to the relative weight accorded to *abhinaya* as compared with *nṛtta*, or abstract dance. In Kathākali, for example, which is basically a form of dance drama, the emphasis is almost exclusively on *abhinaya*,[21] while in Bharata Nāṭyam in its solo form almost equal emphasis is given to pure dance or *nṛtta*, and representational-cum-expressive dance, or *abhinaya* (see Frontispiece and Color Plates I-VIII). The term *nṛtya*, which is usually defined as the representational element in classical dance as distinguished from *nṛtta*, or the abstract, non-representational element, has come to be used interchangeably with the term *abhinaya*.[22] The term *nāṭya* is also often employed, referring to the element of story line, plot, or drama in dance.[23] Three additional pairs of concepts can now be introduced with regard to Indian dance in general. First, a distinction is generally made between *tāṇḍava*, a forceful, masculine form of dance, and *lāsya*, a lyrical, graceful feminine form--usually but by no means exclusively, to be performed by men and women, respectively.[24] Second, two modes of acting or *abhinaya* are recognized: *nāṭyadharmī*, a purely conventional mode of representation in drama and dance, and *lokadharmī*, realistic or naturalistic imitation of real life situations.[25] Finally, forms of drama and dance are classified into *mārgī* (literally, of the path), and *deśī* (literally, of a region). The closest Western equivalents of *mārgī* and *deśī* are "classical," and "popular" or "folk," respectively. A *mārgī* form is based on Sanskrit *śāstras* or technical treatises on the arts and sciences, such as the *Nāṭyaśāstra*. It is technically highly evolved and is governed by strict rules and conventions of performance. Its mastery requires native talent, long years of training, and a superior degree of discipline. A *deśī* form is relatively informal, easy to master, employs a vernacular language or languages whenever appropriate, rather than Sanskrit, and is generally light and entertaining in nature and thus has popular appeal.[26]

Of all the *rasas*, *śṛṅgāra rasa* has probably been the most frequently exemplified in the arts of India. Because of its dominant role, it has been exhaustively analyzed and commented upon in numerous treatises on aesthetics, as well as in those dealing with specific arts, such as dramaturgy, dance, and poetics, from the time of the author of the *Nāṭyaśāstra* to the present day. *Śṛṅgāra rasa* has been traditionally divided into *vipralambha śṛṅgāra*, love in separation, and *saṃbhoga śṛṅgāra*, love in fulfillment or enjoyment.[27] Of the two, love in separation offers a greater range of possibilities of expression in drama and dance, since it is subject to a greater variety of dominant emotions and transitory emotional states. Hence *vipralambha śṛṅgāra* has received much more attention than has *saṃbhoga śṛṅgāra* in treatises on the performing arts. Ten stages of love in separation or unfulfilled love are commonly recognized in the *śāstras*. They are: *ābhilāsa*, longing; *cintā*, anxiety; *anusmṛti*, recollection (of the beloved); *guṇakīrtana*, enumeration of (the beloved's) merits; *udvega*, distress; *vilāpa*, lamentation; *unmāda*, insanity; *vyādhi*, sickness; *jaḍatā*, stupor; *maraṇa*, death. In drama and dance, tradition prohibits the representation of the last stage.[28]

In the literature dealing with *śṛṅgāra rasa* a variety of classifications have been devised of the *nāyaka* and *nāyikā*, or hero and heroine in love, the *dūta* and *dūtī*, their male and female messengers, and the *sakhī*, the heroine's female companion, confidante, and go-between. The most detailed treatment has been accorded to the *nāyikā*. She has been classified according to whether she belongs to the hero, belongs to another, or belongs to anyone (i.e., is a courtesan); according to whether she is young and naive, adolescent and in the early stages of experiencing love, or mature and experienced; according to whether she is superior, middling, or inferior in character as evidenced in her behavior toward her lover, etc., etc. The most widely recognized classification of the *nāyikā* is based on eight situations in which she may find herself. She is *vāsakasajjā*, when dressed and adorned in expectation of her lover's arrival; *virahotkaṇṭhitā*, when distressed at her lover's absence; *svādhīnapatikā* or *svādhīnabhartṛkā*, when her lover stays by her side and is in her power; *kalahāntaritā*, when estranged from her lover because of a quarrel; *khaṇḍitā*, when enraged because her lover has gone to meet another woman; *vipralabdhā*, when her lover does not appear for the tryst; *proṣitabhartṛkā*, when her lover has gone abroad on a journey; and *abhisārikā*, when, lovesick, she throws all modesty and caution to the winds and hurries to a tryst with her lover.[29]

It is noteworthy that seven out of eight of the above circumstances in which the *nāyikā* finds herself are cases of love in separation, the one exception being the *svādhīnapatikā* or *svādhīnabhartṛkā* case, which represents love in enjoyment--thus illustrating the point that *vipralambha śṛṅgāra* is a theme richer in possibilities of *abhinaya* than is *saṃbhoga śṛṅgāra*.

Anomg important characteristics of the *nāyikā,* as portrayed in drama and dance, are *sāttvika alaṃkāras,* or natural graces of women, which include beauty of form and character, and *hāvas,* or amorous gestures, whether spontaneous or deliberate. Examples of the beauty of form or character are: *śobhā*, beauty; *kānti*, loveliness; *dīpti*, radiance; *mādhurya*, sweetness. Spontaneous amorous gestures are exemplified by (spontaneous manifestation of): *vilāsa*, delight; *vibhrama*, confusion; *kilakiñcita*, hysteria. Examples of deliberate amorous gestures are: *līlā*, playfulness; *lalita*, lolling (implying a graceful pose); *kuṭṭamita*, pretending anger; *bibboka*, affecting indifference.[30]

I will now focus on some general characteristics of Bharata Nāṭyam.[31] As was pointed out earlier, in Bharata Nāṭyam approximately equal weight is accorded to pure dance (*nṛtta*) and representational-cum-expressive dance (*abhinaya*). While in *nṛtta* many factors--such as the vitality and grace of the artiste, the splendor of costume, the formal perfection of poses, gestures and patterns of movement, the precision and rhythmic complexity of footwork--all contribute to the evocation of aesthetic delight in the audience, it is *abhinaya* alone which conveys *rasa*, in the strict sense of the evocation of aesthetic moods based on dominant emotions (*sthāyi bhāvas*) and transitory emotional states (*sañcāri bhāvas*). The following discussion will deal mainly with the *abhinaya* component of Bharata Nāṭyam. (For a discussion of *nṛtta* see Chapter III.)

As an art form, Bharata Nāṭyam is based on a tradition of performances in temples, at religious festivals, at royal courts, and at weddings and other functions in the homes of wealthy patrons. This mixed religious and secular heritage is reflected in the various *abhinaya* items of its standard repertory. Thus, for example, the praise of a god or king is the major theme of a *śabdam*, while a love lyric addressed to a deity, mythological hero, or royal patron may constitute the theme of a *varṇam, svarajati*, *padam*, or *jāvali*.[32] The link between the religious and the secular is provided by *śṛṅgāra rasa*, the mood most often evoked in Bharata Nāṭyam. Since, in its solo form--the form which concerns us here--Bharata Nāṭyam is usually performed by a woman, in the tradition of the *devadāsī*, *rājadāsī*, and *alaṃkāradāsī*,[33] she, naturally, most frequently impersonates the traditional *nāyikā* in love with a god, a deified hero, or a king.

The types of *nāyikā*, her situations, stages of love in separation, natural graces, and amorous gestures, have all been the themes of numerous *padams* and *jāvalis*. In case the object of the *nāyikā's* love is human, the theme of the *abhinaya* item which portrays it is *śṛṅgāra rasa*, in the literal sense of human love between the sexes. If, on the other hand, the beloved is divine, then the literal level of meaning signifies (represents, symbolizes) the human soul's striving for union with God, and thus its theme is ultimately that of *madhura bhakti*, or *śṛṅgāra bhakti*--passionate love of God.[34] Furthermore, in these latter situations the *nāyikā* represents the human soul, whether it be that of a man or a woman; for, according to the Bhakti tradition, the devotee of a male deity is most adequately represented as feminine in relation to the god worshipped, regardless of the worshipper's gender.[35]

The Bharata Nāṭyam dancer employs *āṅgika abhinaya* and *sāttvika abhinaya* to convey *bhāva* and evoke *rasa*. *Āhārya*, which comprises costume, makeup and jewelry, does not figure as an element in *abhinaya* in this case, since it does not vary with each specific theme, role, or emotional situation enacted. Rather, its function is purely decorative. *Vācika abhinaya*, or expression through words and song, currently devolves exclusively on the vocalists in the dancer's ensemble of musicians.

In *āṅgika abhinaya* the means of communication are poses, movements, gestures and facial expressions. The authoritative texts divide the parts of the body into three categories: the *aṅgas*, *pratyaṅgas*, and *upāṅgas*, or major limbs, minor limbs and features, respectively.[36] According to one such classification, the *aṅgas* include the head, neck, hands, chest, sides, waist and feet; the *pratyaṅgas* include the shoulders, shoulder blades, arms, back, thighs, and calves; the *upāṅgas* include the face, eyes, eyebrows, eyelids, pupils, cheeks, nose, jaws, lips, teeth, tongue, and chin. The appendages to the *upāṅgas* consist of the palms, fingers, ankles, heels, toes, and the insides of the feet. All of these play a role in pure as well as in representational-cum-expressive dance; however, in the latter the dancer communicates primarily through facial expressions and hand gestures.

Hasta mudrās, or hand gestures, commonly simply referred to as *hastas*, are divided into *asaṃyuta hastas*, hand gestures of the single hand; and *saṃyuta hastas*, hand gestures of both hands combined. The *hastas* are also divided into *nṛtta hastas*, hand gestures employed in pure dance, to which no meanings are assigned and whose function is purely decorative; and *abhinaya hastas*, hand gestures employed in representational-cum-expressive dance, each of which is capable of communicating a range of meanings known as *viniyogas*--literally, uses--the particular meaning intended in a given instance being determined by context. For example, in Colorplate V both hands are in the *asaṃyuta hasta padmakośa* (lotus bud), joined at the wrists while the fingers open outwards, symbolizing an opening lotus--a frequent image employed in *abhinaya*, intended literally, metaphorically, or as a simile. The *asaṃyuta hasta patāka* (flag), illustrated in Colorplate I, functions purely as an ornament in *nṛtta*, but is capable of communicating a range of meanings or *viniyogas* in the context of *abhinaya*. According to one text, these meanings are: clouds, forest, bosom, night, river, moonlight, sea waves, rainy day, prowess, shallow pool, height, wall, dwarf, shade of tree, mirror, to enter a street, to anoint the body, to take an oath, to touch, to sweep, to condemn, to lie down, to deny, to defend, to level, to slap, to spread.[37]

In the context of Bharata Nāṭyam *sāttvika abhinaya* does *not* mean -- as it does in the *Nāṭyaśāstra* -- "imitation of involuntary expressions of emotional states" such as weeping, trembling, fainting, etc. The latter are communicated through the appropriate *hastas* and/or suggested through facial expressions. The employment of *sāttvika abhinaya* in Bharata Nāṭyam consists in the infusing of soul, life and feeling into the performance, and imbuing it with subtlety and suggestion evocative of *rasa*.[38] Furthermore, in Bharata Nāṭyam the *sañcāri_bhāva* technique concerns more than the mere portrayal of transitory emotional states as facets of a dominant emotion. It also involves the rendering, by means of *āṅgika* and *sāttvika abhinaya*, of a line, phrase, or even word of a poetic text in a variety of ways, each rendition bringing out a different connotation, nuance of meaning, or mode of expressive or dramatic realization of the subject represented.[39] Thus, for example, a line such as "O Kṛṣṇa, I long for you" may be rendered five times in a given *abhinaya* item, Kṛṣṇa being represented each time as the actor in a different episode, such as playing the flute, dancing on the hoods of the serpent Kāliya, holding Mt. Govardhana aloft on his little finger, etc.;

while the *nāyikā's* longing for him may be represented by the dancer's walking about and looking round in all directions longingly, writing a letter presumably addressed to Kṛṣṇa, sitting on the floor with an attitude and expression of despondency alternating with hope, etc. The range of possibilities of interpretation is virtually inexhaustible, limited only by the dancer's own limitations in erudition, resourcefulness and sensitivity.

The effective employment of *sāttvika abhinaya* and the *sañcāri bhāva* technique is a measure of the dancer's stature as an artist; for, far beyond the mastery of technique, it depends on her knowledge of the literary tradition, vitality, emotional maturity, and creative imagination, as well as self-forgetful involvement in the performance.

Since *abhinaya* items in Bharata Nāṭyam focus mainly on the *nāyikā* in love, the *lāsya,* or feminine style of dance, predominates. However, in the course of expounding her theme the dancer is frequently required to impersonate the object of her love, i.e., typically, a king, a hero, or a male deity; on those latter occasions the *tāṇḍava*, or masculine style of dance is, of course, the appropriate one.

The mode of acting in Bharata Nāṭyam is predominantly *nāṭyadharmī*--governed by conventions of representation on the stage rather than realistic imitation of life. The employment of an elaborate language of stylized hand gestures; the solo dancer's impersonation of different characters in the same story; retaining the same costume while assuming different dramatic roles; changes of facial expression in rapid, kaleidoscopic succession to indicate transitory moods and emotional states; communicating involuntary expressions of emotions, such as weeping, by hand gestures, rather than actually exhibiting them--all these are non-realistic features of the *abhinaya* tradition. Attitudes of the body and facial expressions, however, do contribute a realistic element (*lokadharmī*) to the mode of acting in Bharata Nāṭyam. Thus, for example, when the expression of sadness or grief is called for, bowed head, lowered eyelids, mouth turned down at the corners, are all appropriate and do imitate real life. These elements in *abhinaya* have a direct appeal to an uninitiated audience because their appreciation does not depend on a knowledge of the language of *hastas*. The emphasis accorded to them in Bharata Nāṭyam varies from school to school and from performer to performer. However, by and large, *nāṭyadharmī* elements predominate.

Bharata Nāṭyam is a technically highly developed performing art, rich in the vocabulary and syntax of pure as well as representational dance, incorporating classical Carnatic music as its melodic and rhythmic dimensions. It is, of course, also based on *śāstraic* literature devoted wholly or in part to dance--such as the *Nāṭyaśāstra*, the *Abhinayadarpaṇam* of Nandikeśvara, and the *Saṅgītaratnākara* of Śārṅgadeva.[40] Hence it is a *mārgī* art form. However, it should not be forgotten that the Bhakti movement and its influence on temple worship has played a vital role in the development of Bharata Nāṭyam. Bhakti was, in essence, a movement of wide popular appeal. Its intense religious devotionalism addressed itself to everyone, regardless of caste distinctions. Indeed, some *bhakti* saints were themselves untouchables.[41] The popular character of the movement is reflected in the songs whose simple lyrics were composed in the vernacular--Tamil, Telugu, and Kannada--by *bhakti* poet-saints. It is these songs, originally sung and interpreted in *abhinaya* by *devadāsīs* serving in temples, which comprise a large part of the musical and poetic repertory of Bharata Nāṭyam. They constitute a *deśī* element in the dance tradition.

There is, however, a *deśī* trend in a different sense which has recently been creeping into Bharata Nāṭyam, introduced by teachers as well as performers. While in the past dance performances in the Bharata Nāṭyam tradition took place primarily in temples and royal palaces, before images of deities and/or audiences of connoisseurs, today they take place in theaters and auditoria, before large audiences of mixed background, in India and abroad. There has been a corresponding trend towards popularization, i.e., simplification of rhythm, increasing emphasis on the *lokadharmī* mode of *abhinaya*, etc. In the opinion of connoisseurs, this tendency to appeal to the lowest common denominator of comprehension and sensibility has inevitably resulted in a decline in artistic standards. They acknowledge, however, that there are still some few *gurus* and performing artists who are committed to the transmission to future generations of standards of technical perfection, purity of form, and the range and subtlety of expression which traditionally has been the hallmark of Bharata Nāṭyam at its best.[42]

Notes

1. Bharata Muni, *The Nāṭyaśāstra*, edited and translated by Manomohan Ghosh. Text: vol. I (Calcutta: Manisha Granthalaya Private Limited, 1967); vol. II (Calcutta, 1956). Translation: 2nd rev. ed., vol. I (Calcutta: Manisha Granthalaya Private Limited, 1967); vol. II (Calcutta: The Asiatic Society, 1961).

2. Edwin Gerow, *Indian Poetics* (Wiesbaden: Otto Harrassowitz, 1977), p. 225 & n. 33; p. 245.

3. *Nāṭyaśāstra*, I: 7-23.

4. Ibid., IV: 13-14. All of Chapter IV is devoted to dance.

5. For a translation of Chapter VI of the *Nāṭyaśāstra*, and of excerpts from Abhinavagupta's commentary, the *Abhinavabhāratī*, as well as the editors' detailed explanatory notes, see J. L. Masson and M.V. Patwardhan, *Aesthetic Rapture: The Rasâdhyāya of the Nāṭyaśāstra*, in two volumes (Poona: Deccan College Postgraduate and Research Institute, 1970).

6. The standard histories are P.V. Kane, *History of Sanskrit Poetics*, 3rd rev. ed. (Delhi: Motilal Banarsidass, 1961); and S. K. De, *History of Sanskrit Poetics*, 2nd rev. ed. (Calcutta: Firma K.L. Mukhopadhyay, 1960). For a succinct survey, see Gerow, *Indian Poetics*. Also, see "General Introduction," in D.H. Ingalls, *An Anthology of Sanskrit Court Poetry* (Cambridge, Massachusetts: Harvard University Press, 1965), pp. 1-53; and V. Raghavan and Nagendra, eds., *An Introduction to Indian Poetics* (Bombay: Macmillan and Company Limited, 1970).

7. See Ānandavardhana, *Dhvanyāloka*, edited and translated by K. Krishnamoorthy (Delhi: Motilal Banarsidass, 1982). *Dhvanyāloka* of Ānandavardhana, edited with the *Dhvanyāloka Locana* of Abhinavagupta by Durgaprasad Shastri (Bombay: Kāvyamālā, Nirṇayasāgara Press, 1890). For translations of relevant passages by Abhinavagupta, see Raniero Gnoli, *The Aesthetic Experience According to Abhinavagupta* (Varanasi: The Chowkhamba Sanskrit Series Office, 1968); J. L. Masson and M.V. Patwardhan, *Śāntarasa and Abhinavagupta's Philosophy of Aesthetics* (Poona: Bhandarkar Oriental Research Institute, 1969), and *Aesthetic Rapture*. Also, see K.C. Pandey, *Abhinavagupta: An Historical and Philosophical Study*, 2nd ed. (Varanasi: Chowkhamba, 1966). The most recent (as of 1990) and by far the best translation of Ānandavardhana and Abhinavagupta is *The Dhvanyāloka of Ānandavardhana with the Locana of Abhinavagupta*, translated by Daniel H. H. Ingalls, Jeffrey Moussaieff Mason, and M.V. Patwardhan; edited with an introduction by Daniel H. H. Ingalls (Cambridge, Massachusetts: Harvard University Press, 1990).

8. *Nāṭyaśāstra*, VI: 17; VII. 7-27.

9. See V. Raghavan, *The Number of Rasas*, 3rd rev. ed. (Madras: The Adyar Library and Research Centre, 1975), pp. 77-83.

10. *Nāṭyaśāstra*, VI: 18-21; VII. 27-93.
11. Both Ānandavardhana and Abhinavagupta provide extensive discussions of the role of suggestion in the evocation of *rasa*. (Ānandavardhana's term designating suggestion is *dhvani*, literally, "resonance.") Cf. works cited in note 7.
12. Ibid., VI: 22; VII. 93-106.
13. Ibid., VIII: 1-9.
14. For a lucid exposition of the concept of *rasa*, see Mysore Hiriyanna, *Art Experience* (Mysore: Kavyalaya Publishers, 1954), pp. 25-42. Also, cf. Masson and Patwardhan, *Aesthetic Rapture*; Raghavan, *The Number of Rasas*.
15. The impersonality of the *rasa* experience is expressed in Abhinavagupta by the term *sādhāraṇīkaraṇa* (literally, universalization). See Gnoli, *The Aesthetic Experience*, p. 44; Masson and Patwardhan, *Śāntarasa*, pp. 72, n. 3; 74, n. 2.
16. Ibid., p. 158; cf. Hiriyanna, *Art Experience*, pp. 25-28.
17. *Nāṭyaśāstra*, VI; cf. Masson and Patwardhan, *Aesthetic Rapture*, and *Śāntarasa*.
18. Cf. Gerow, *Indian Poetics*, p. 245 and seq.
19. For Abhinavagupta's definition of the term *sahṛdaya*, see Masson and Patwardhan, *Śāntarasa*, p. 78, n. 4.
20. For an excellent introduction to the major classical dance traditions of India, see Mohan Khokar, *Traditions of Indian Classical Dance*, 2nd rev. ed. (New Delhi: Clarion Books, 1984).
21. Ibid., pp. 94-129.
22. Ibid., pp. 77-78.
23. Ibid., p. 58.
24. Ibid., p. 59.
25. *Nāṭyaśāstra*, VI: 24. Also see V. Raghavan, "Nāṭyadharmī and Lokadharmī," *Journal of Oriental Research*, VII, no. 4 (October-December 1933), pp. 359-375; VIII, no. 1 (January-March 1934), pp. 57-74.
26. See Khokar, loc. cit., p. 59.
27. *Nāṭyaśāstra*, VI: 44-45.
28. *Nāṭyaśāstra*, XXIV: 169-191.
29. *Nāṭyaśāstra*, XXIV: 210-219. For a detailed, systematic treatment of the *Nāyaka*, *Nāyikā* and related concepts in Indian tradition, see Rākeśagupta, *Studies in Nāyaka-Nāyikā-Bheda* (Aligarh: Granthayan, 1967).
30. Ibid., pp. 376-381.
31. For a general introduction to Bharata Nāṭyam, see Khokar, loc. cit., pp. 72-93. For a more detailed account, see Mrinalini Sarabhai, *Understanding Bharata Natyam* (Ahmedabad: The Darpana Academy of Performing Arts, 1981). Also, cf. Kapila Vatsyayan, *Indian Classical Dance* (New Delhi: Publications Division, Ministry of Information and Broadcasting, Government of India, 1974), pp. 1-24. Mohan Khokar's *Dancing Bharata Natyam* (Bombay: Bharatiya Vidya Bhavan, 1979) deals exclusively with *aḍavus*, the basic units of pure dance (*nṛtta*).

32. For a description of individual items in the Bharata Nāṭyam repertory, see Chapter I. Also, cf. E. Krishna Iyer, "Repertoire: Alarippu to Tillana," in Sunil Kothari, ed., *Bharata Natyam: Indian Classical Dance* Art (Bombay: Marg Publications, 1979), pp. 83-92.

33. See Chapter I.

34. Raghavan, *The Number of Rasas*, pp. 142-143.

35. See A.K. Ramanujan, *Hymns for the Drowning* (Princeton, New Jersey: Princeton University Press, 1981), pp. 153-154.

36. *Nāṭyaśāstra*, VIII: 11-13; also, see Sarabhai, op. cit., p. 72.

37. Cf. Nandikeśvara, *Abhinayadarpaṇam*, edited and translated by Manomohan Ghosh, 3rd ed. (Calcutta: Manisha Granthalaya Private Limited, 1975), pp. 48-63. Also, see Sarabhai, op. cit., pp. 85-122.

38. See Khokar, *Traditions of Indian Classical Dance*, p. 63.

39. Ibid., p. 67.

40. Śārṅgadeva, *Saṅgītaratnākara of Śārṅgadeva*, Sanskrit text and English translation by R. K. Shringy, vols. 1-2 (Delhi: Motilal Banarsidass, 1978-1989).

41. For a highly perceptive, sensitive account of the early Bhakti movement in Tamil Nadu, see Ramanujan, op. cit., pp. 103-169.

42. Cf. Milton Singer, *When a Great Tradition Modernizes* (New York: Praeger Publishers, 1972), pp. 172-182.

Bibliography

Ānandavardhana, *Dhvanyāloka*, edited and translated by K. Krishnamoorthy (Delhi: Motilal Banarsidass, 1982).

Ānandavardhana, *Dhvanyāloka*, edited with the *Dhvanyāloka Locana* of Abhinavagupta by Durgaprasad Shastri (Bombay: Kāvyamālā, Nirṇayasāgara Press, 1890).

Ānandavardhana and Abhinavagupta, *The Dhvanyāloka of Ānandavardhana with the Locana of Abhinavagupta,* translated by Daniel H. H. Ingalls, Jeffrey Moussaieff Mason, and M.V. Patwardhan; edited with an introduction by Daniel H. H. Ingalls (Cambridge, Massachusetts: Harvard University Press, 1990).

Bharata Muni, *The Nāṭyaśāstra*, edited and translated by Manomohan Ghosh. Text: vol. I (Calcutta: Manisha Granthalaya Private Limited, 1967); vol. II (Calcutta, 1956). Translation: 2nd rev. ed., vol. I (Calcutta: Manisha Granthalaya Private Limited, 1967); vol. II (Calcutta: The Asiatic Society, 1961).

De, S. K., *History of Sanskrit Poetics,* 2nd rev. ed. (Calcutta: Firma K.L. Mukhopadhyay, 1960).

Gerow, Edwin, *Indian Poetics* (Wiesbaden: Otto Harrassowitz, 1977).

Gnoli, Raniero, *The Aesthetic Experience According to Abhinavagupta* (Varanasi: The Chowkhamba Sanskrit Series Office, 1968).

Hiriyanna, Mysore, *Art Experience* (Mysore: Kavyalaya Publishers, 1954).

Ingalls, D.H., *An Anthology of Sanskrit Court Poetry* (Cambridge, Massachusetts: Harvard University Press, 1965).

Iyer, E. Krishna, "Repertoire: Alarippu to Tillana," in Sunil Kothari, ed., *Bharata Natyam: Indian Classical Dance Art* (Bombay: Marg Publications, 1979), pp. 83-92.

Kane, P.V., *History of Sanskrit Poetics*, 3rd rev. ed. (Delhi: Motilal Banarsidass, 1961).

Khokar, Mohan, *Dancing Bharata Natyam* (Bombay: Bharatiya Vidya Bhavan, 1979).

Khokar, Mohan, *Traditions of Indian Classical Dance*, 2nd rev. ed. (New Delhi: Clarion Books, 1984).

Masson, J.L. and Patwardhan, M.V., *Aesthetic Rapture: The Rasâdhyāya of the Nāṭyaśāstra*, in two volumes (Poona: Deccan College Postgraduate and Research Institute, 1970).

Masson, J.L. and Patwardhan, M.V., *Śāntarasa and Abhinavagupta's Philosophy of Aesthetics*, (Poona: Bhandarkar Oriental Research Institute, 1969).

Nandikeśvara, *Abhinayadarpaṇam*, edited and translated by Manomohan Ghosh, 3rd ed. (Calcutta: Manisha Granthalaya Private Limited, 1975).

Pandey, K.C., *Abhinavagupta: An Historical and Philosophical Study*, 2nd ed. (Varanasi: Chowkhamba, 1966).

Raghavan, V., "Nāṭyadharmī and Lokadharmī," *Journal of Oriental Research*, VII, No. 4 (October-December 1933), pp. 359-375; VIII, No. 1 (January-March 1934), pp. 57-74.

Raghavan, V., *The Number of Rasas*, 3rd rev. ed. (Madras: The Adyar Library and Research Centre, 1975).

Raghavan, V. and Nagendra, eds., *An Introduction to Indian Poetics* (Bombay: Macmillan and Company Limited, 1970).

Rākeśagupta, *Studies in Nāyaka-Nāyikā-Bheda* (Aligarh: Granthayan, 1967).

Ramanujan, A.K., *Hymns for the Drowning* (Princeton, New Jersey: Princeton University Press, 1981)

Śārṅgadeva, *Saṅgītaratnākara of Śārṅgadeva*, Sanskrit text and English translation by R. K. Shringy, vols. 1-2 (Delhi: Motilal Banarsidass, 1978-1989).

Sarabhai, Mrinalini, *Understanding Bharta Natyam* (Ahmedabad: The Darpana Academy of Performing Arts, 1981).

Singer, Milton, *When a Great Tradition Modernizes* (New York: Praeger Publishers, 1972).

Vatsyayan, Kapila, *Indian Classical Dance* (New Delhi: Publications Division, Ministry of Information and Broadcasting, Government of India, 1974).

III

Characteristics of *Nṛtta* in Bharata Nāṭyam[1]

Judy Van Zile

Written Theory of *Nṛtta*

Bharata Nāṭyam dance that has no specific narrative meaning is known as *nṛtta*. *Nṛtta* is often referred to as "pure" or "abstract" dance, and utilizes complex rhythmic movement to display the beauty of the body in motion.

A number of treatises exist on theory of *nṛtta*. The most frequently cited is the *Nāṭyaśāstra*, an encyclopedic Sanskrit work written sometime between the second century B.C. and the fourth century A.D. Although this voluminous work is usually attributed to Bharata Muni, it is more likely that portions written at various times by several authors were eventually compiled into a single work.

The Sanskrit text is an exposition on drama. But because the concepts of dance and drama were not separate in ancient India, a wealth of information is included on dance. Topics relating to dance range from appropriate emotional moods to be conveyed to music, costumes, and details on the use of the body.

Over the centuries several commentaries have been written on the *Nāṭyśāstra*; the most widely known is the *Abhinavabhāratī*, by Abhinavagupta. Additionally, portions of the *Nāṭyaśāstra* have been published separately, such as the fourth chapter, known as *Tāṇḍavalakṣaṇam*, and many independent treatises dealing with dance theory have been written, such as *Abhinayadarpaṇam* by Nandikeśvara, and *Saṅgītaratnākara*, by Śārṅgadeva. Some of these texts simply restate the original material contained in the *Nāṭyaśāstra*, some attempt to clarify and comment on the original material, and some establish their own systems for classifying and describing dance movements.

The movement theory set forth in the *Nāṭyaśāstra* is extremely complex, so it is understandable that subsequent writers attempted to explain the intent of the original volume. One classification system set forth is based on movements of different parts of the body. Major limbs--identified as *aṅgas*--include the head, hands, breast, waist, hips, and feet. Minor limbs--*upāṅga*--include the eyes, eyebrows, nose, lips, chin, and mouth. Fixed numbers of positions (*sthānaka*), gaits (*cārīs*), and hand gestures (*hasta mudrās*[2]) are described.

Another classification system is based on combinations of movements of the major and minor limbs, and these are described at various levels and assigned specific terms.

Of these terms, one of the most widely known is *karaṇa*. It has frequently been defined as a static pose that forms the basis for larger units of movement. Vatsyayan,[3] however, believes *karaṇas* are "arrested moments" from sequences of movement--the *karaṇas* depicted in sculpture capturing the culminating pose.

Sculptures found on temples, particularly the Bṛhadīśvara Temple in Tanjore (built in the eleventh century), and the Naṭarāja Temple in Cidambaram (see Chapter V, Plates 7 and 8) in the state of Tamil Nadu (built in the fourteenth century), depict the 108 *karaṇas* described in the *Nāṭyaśāstra*. Sculptures on the east and west gates of the temple in Cidambaram include the relevant portion of the

Nāṭyaśāstra text incised beneath the posture depicted. The following are examples of verses from the *Nāṭyaśāstra* that describe *karaṇas*.

> Samanakha--the two Samankha [*sic*] feet touching each other, two hands hanging down, and the body in a natural pose.
>
> Līna--the two Patāka hands held together in Añjali pose on the chest, the neck held high, and the shoulder bent.
>
> Svastikarecita--two hands with Recita and Āviddha gesture held together in the form of a Svastika, then separated and held on the hip. [4]

Larger units of movement are created by joining together various *karaṇas*. The *Nāṭyaśāstra* describes several "levels" of movement combinations as follows.

> The combined [movement of] hands and feet in dance is called the Karaṇa: Two Karaṇas will make one Mātṛkā, and two, three, or four Mātṛkās will make up one Aṅgahāra. Three Karaṇas will make a Kalāpaka, four a Śaṇḍaka, and five a Saṃghātaka. Thus the Aṅgahāras consist of six, seven, eight or nine Karaṇas.[5]

The unit of movement most frequently identified by Bharata Nāṭyam dancers today is the *aḍavu*. This movement unit will first be described in general, and then detailed explanations of several examples will serve as the basis for generalizations about pure dance technique in Bharata Nāṭyam.

Aḍavus: *Aḍavu* Groups

The *aḍavu* is

> a short movement phrase (or identifiable unit of movement) which, when linked with other phrases, forms a dance. There are approximately twelve different sequences traditionally identified as *aṭavu* [*sic*.] groups . . ., the precise number dependent on the historical treatise (e.g., *Nāṭyaśāstra*), teacher, or performer consulted. *Aṭavus* are comprised primarily of three components: (1) movements of the arms and legs; (2) *mudrās* (fixed positions of the fingers or hand gestures that move from one position to another); and (3) limited movement of the torso and head.
>
> . . .
>
> Each *aṭavu* has a number of prescribed variants, the *aṭavu* and its variants together sometimes being referred to as an *aṭavu* group. Although performance details of each *aṭavu* and its variants may differ between teachers or performers, within each teacher's style they are set. New *aṭavus* or variants are not created. Rather, the traditional units of movement are combined in different ways to create dance pieces.[6]

Although the number of *aḍavu* groups and precise nature of the variants differ, (as do the number of *hastas*), the movement differences in the variations are minor, and characteristics may be delineated that clearly identify the pure dance technique of Bharata Nāṭyam.

Besides forming the motifs from which pure dance is choreographed, *aḍavus* serve as basic exercise patterns that are practiced by the dancer. When doing so she recites a series of mnemonic syllables that aid her in maintaining her rhythmic patters. An *aḍavu* group is often identified by the syllables to which it is performed, or by related syllables assigned to identify the *aḍavu* group. The dancer practices the *aḍavus* at three speeds, the second doubling that of the first, and the third quadrupling that of the first.

A general description of two *aḍavu* groups will serve as a basis for describing the major movement characteristics of pure dance in Bharata Nāṭyam. (The reader should keep in mind that it is not possible to learn dance movements from verbal descriptions or illustrations. These forms of documentation are provided here only to suggest the nature of the movements, so that the generalizations described later will be meaningful. For the dance specialist, the appendix contains Labanotation scores of the second *aḍavu* group described. These scores include a greater level of specificity in detailing movement sequences than the verbal descriptions and illustrations because of the ease of including such detail in Labanotation.)

Aḍavus: Taṭṭu Aḍavu

The dancer begins her practice with an *aḍavu* group known as *taṭṭu aḍavu*, the name derived from a word meaning "to strike flat," or "to slap." With her feet together, legs outwardly rotated so knees and toes point as directly to the sides as possible, and knees deeply bent (while still keeping the heels on the floor--see Figure 1), she executes a flat-footed stamp that creates a crisp "slap" on the floor and causes the bells on her ankles to resound. Each variant within this *aḍavu* group increases the number of stamps and/or changes the rhythmic pattern of the stamps. Figure 2 shows the rhythmic patterns of the variants within this *aḍavu* group learned by the writer from Balasaraswati (1918-1984), one of the foremost exponents of Bharata Nāṭyam.[7]

The basic motif is a single stamp. This is done with the right foot, but the motif may then be repeated with the left foot. In the first variant two stamps are executed on the right foot in an even rhythmic pattern. The second and third variants simply increase the number of stamps to three and four respectively, still retaining the even, rhythmic structure. In the fourth and fifth variants one stamp is added to each, and the rhythmic pattern is changed in each. And the final variant is a combination of variant four immediately followed by variant five. In each variant all stamps are performed with the same foot, but the pattern may then be repeated with the opposite foot.

Although the isolated stamping patterns found in this *aḍavu* group would not appear in a dance, they serve as exercises that help the performer develop the correct way of executing the stamp--which is used in other *aḍavu* groups--and contribute to the development of flexibility in rhythmic execution of movement. (Because this sequence functions solely as an exercise, no specific arm gestures are used. The backs of the hands may rest on the hips, as in Figure 1, or the arms may be extended sideward at shoulder height, as in Figure 3.)

The variants in this *aḍavu* group show one of the predominant features of pure dance in the items of the concert repertoire: the use of variety by elaborating on a basic motif. In this instance variety is achieved in two ways: by adding to the original motif, and by modifying the rhythmic pattern of the original motif.

Aḍavus: Naṭṭu Aḍavu

The next *aḍavu* group is known as *naṭṭu aḍavu*, the name derived from *naṭṭu*, meaning "to stretch." In it the dancer begins to more fully vary the movement of the legs, to travel through space, and to use arm movements. Variants within this group, as taught by Balasaraswati, will now be described.

Basic Motif. The dancer begins in the same position as in the *taṭṭu aḍavu* group--feet together, legs outwardly rotated as much as possible, and knees deeply bent. The arms extend to the sides at shoulder height, are slightly bent, and are rotated inward so the elbows are lifted and the palms face down (see Figure 3). The hands are in *tripatāka* (see Figure 4a). The sequence progresses as follows (see Figure 5).

count 1 Right leg extends to the right side, knee straight, heel contacting the floor, ankle bent at a right angle. Right arm rotates outward so the palm faces up, with the elbow extended. Head turns to look at the right hand.

count 2 Right leg returns to its starting position with a stamp, and right arm turns inward and bends to return to its starting position. Head returns to its starting position.

The basic motif comprises two counts.

Variant One. The First variant is achieved by adding movement to the end of the motif, as follows (see Figure 6):

counts 1-4 Basic motif to the right and left.

count 5 Ball of the right foot stamps behind the left foot. Right elbow bends so the lower arm is drawn in directly in front of the chest, palm facing upward. Gaze is lowered to focus on the right hand.

count 6 Without lifting the body, the weight is taken very briefly on the ball of the right foot so the left foot can be lifted and execute a flat-footed stamp on the same spot where it has been. Right arm and gaze remain where they are.

count 7 Right foot and right arm extend to the right side as in count 1. Head turns to focus on the right hand.

count 8 Right foot closes and stamps as in count 2. Right arm turns over and bends to return to its starting position. Head returns to looking directly forward.

In this variant the basic motif has been expanded by adding a small unit of movement (counts 5-6), and by repeating the basic motif (a total of 2 executions at the beginning of the variant, and 1 at the end). The rhythmic pattern of the basic motif has been maintained--the regular execution of a movement on each metrical beat. Variety is achieved solely by the addition of movement. The overall pattern may be stated as

A to the right side
A to the left side
B
A to the right side.

Variant Two. The second variant contains the same number of counts as the first variant. It starts with the original motif, but adds different patterns than those found in variant one (see Figure 7).

counts 1-4	Basic motif to the right and left.
count 5	Right leg extends forward, knee straight, heel contacting the floor, and ankle bent at a right angle. Torso twists 1/4 counterclockwise so left arm points toward the back. Right arm straightens and extends directly forward, palm facing up. Face looks at right hand.
count 6	Weight is taken momentarily on the right foot so the left foot can stamp where it was.
count 7	Right foot stamps alongside of left, torso returns to its normal position, left arm is carried along as torso turns so arm points to left side, right arm bends so upper arm extends to right side and lower arm is directly in front of the chest, palm facing up. Eyes look at right hand.
count 8	Left foot stamps in place.

The overall pattern may be described as

A to the right side
A to the left side
A to the right side
C

The original motif emphasized very flat, two-dimensional movement in a lateral (side-to-side) plane. In this variant the movement continues to be flat, but a change in introduced through the addition of a torso twist to the basic motif (counts 5-6). Instead of the movement being purely side-to-side, the modification to the original motif involves forward-backward movement--movement that emphasizes the sagittal plane.

In this instance variety is achieved by slightly modifying the original motif (counts 5-6), and by adding movement to the original motif (counts 7-8). Additionally, however, the modifications introduce a different use of space (the sagittal plane) than in the basic motif and earlier variant.

Variant Three. The third variant comprises two variations of the basic motif. The dancer begins with feet together, knees bent, and legs outwardly-rotated, as in the original motif. The arms, however, are bent so the hands are close to the front of the chest, palms face each other, and both hands are in *haṃsāsya* (see Figure 4b). The sequence progresses as follows (see Figure 8):

count 1 Right leg extends to right side as in original motif. Torso tilts to right side. Left arm extends upward to left side, right downward to right side. Both hands change to *alapadma* (see Figure 4c), palms facing upward. Face turns to look at right hand.

count 2 Weight is momentarily taken on right leg so left leg can stamp where it was.

count 3 The whole body turns quickly 1/4 counter-clockwise and the dancer steps back onto ball of right foot with knee bent. Torso returns to an upright position. Left arm raises overhead, elbow slightly bent, hand returning to *haṃsāsya* with fingertips pointing to the right side of dancer's body. Right arm extends down behind body, elbow slightly bent, hand returning to *haṃsāsya* with fingertips pointing to left side of dancer's body. Gaze focuses on left hand.

count 4 Weight is momentarily taken on right foot so left foot can stamp where it was. Then pivot quickly 1/4 clockwise on left foot and return to starting position. (The return to the starting position may be eliminated at fast speeds--the dancer simply steps quickly onto the right foot and proceeds to execute the pattern to the left side.)

This variant adds a pivoting, tilting of the torso, and two new hand gestures to the movements of the basic motif and other variants.

Variant Four. Variant four returns to an eight-count phrase (see Figure 9).

counts 1-4 Counts 1-4 of variant 3 to the right side.

count 5 Right leg extends forward with heel contacting floor as in count 5 of variant 2. Torso tilts forward as both arms extend forward and downward, hands changing to *alapadma* with palms facing forward. Gaze focuses on hands.

count 6 Weight is momentarily taken on right so left can stamp where it was.

count 7 Right stamps alongside of left. Torso returns to upright position, and hands return to *haṃsāsya* with arms bent and hands near chest.

count 8 Left foot stamps in place.

This variant begins with variant three, and concludes with a modification of the second part of variant two. It also contains a slight sense of the sagittal plane because of the forward extension of the leg. The tilting of the torso, however, lessens the sagittal emphasis, unlike the clear sagittal sense created in variant two by the forward-backward emphasis in the arms and one leg contrasting with the purely vertical torso.

Variant Five. This variant begins in the same starting position as the previous one--feet together, knees bent, arms bent, with hands in front of the chest in *haṃsāsya*--and proceeds as follows (see Figure 10):

count 1 Jump just slightly off the ground and land in the starting position with a stamp on both feet. Arms extend overhead, hands opening to *alapadma* with palms facing backward. Head tilts slightly back so gaze can focus on hands.

count 2 Right foot stamps to right side, ending with both feet on the ground in a moderate stride with knees bent. Right arm opens out to right side at shoulder height, left to left side at shoulder height. Hand gestures remain, and palms face upward. Gaze focuses on right hand.

count 3 Left foot stamps on ball of foot behind right, knee bent. Torso tilts forward as both arms continue on a circular path until they extend downward, palms facing forward. Hand gestures remain. Gaze focuses on both hands.

count 4 Right foot stamps in place alongside of left, and heel of left foot lowers. Torso returns to upright position, and arms and gaze return to starting position.

This variant adds two new movement elements. First, the arms trace a large circular path rather than taking a straight-line path from one position to another. Second, there is a brief moment when the dancer leaves the ground to perform a jump. But the jump is executed in a manner that does not emphasize height. As the dancer's feet leave the ground she attempts to keep her center of weight the same distance from the floor as when she started--lifting her legs under her rather than lifting her entire body. She lands from the jump with a stamp on both feet, and she may sink into a slightly lower knee-bend than she was in before. Thus, although she leaves the floor it is not the height of the jump that she emphasizes, but the stamp and going down as she lands. In spite of the fact that she has left the ground, the viewer is still aware of a downward emphasis rather than elevation. Again there is a slight suggestion of the sagittal plane because of the forward torso tilt. But this is minimized even more than in variant five because the arms extend directly downward rather than forward toward a gesturing leg.

Variant Six. Variant six is a further modification of variant five, and begins in the same starting position (see Figure 11):

count 1 Jump in place and extend arms overhead as in variant 5.

count 2 Right foot stamps to the right side, ending in a bent-knee stride as in count 2 of variant 5. Arms remain overhead. Hands change to *haṃsāsya* with fingertips pointing forward.

count 3 Stamp on ball of left foot with a bent knee, behind the right foot. Arms begin to open out in a large circular movement that continues from count 3 to count 6. Palms face upward. Both hands open to *alapadma*. Gaze focuses on right hand.

count 4 Right foot stamps to right side, knee bent. Arms continue to open. Hands change to *haṃsāsya* and turn so fingertips point out.

count 5 Stamp on ball of left foot with a bent knee, behind the right foot. Arms continue to open. Both palms face up, hands in *alapadma*. Gaze continues to focus on right hand.

count 6 Right foot stamps to right side, knee bent. Arms arrive extended directly to sides at shoulder height. Hands change to *haṃsāsya* and turn so fingertips point out. Gaze remains on right hand. Arms then return quickly to starting position and left leg moves near to right in preparation for next movement.

count 7 Left foot stamps alongside right, knee bent. Arms extend downward as torso tilts forward. Hands change to *alapadma*, palms facing forward. Gaze focuses on hands.

count 8 Right foot stamps in place. Torso returns to upright position, and arms, hands, and gaze return to starting position.

This variant returns to the flat, lateral movement of the original motif, but elaborates on the circular quality created by the arms in the previous variant. There is a suggestion of the sagittal plane as the torso tilts forward on count seven, but this is minimized by the arms extending directly downward instead of forward, as in variant five.

Two additional variants in the *aḍavu* group recombine movements of the first six variants.

Although the basic motif and variants have been described as starting with the right foot, each is also performed in practice sessions in a laterally symmetrical manner by beginning with the left foot. The laterally symmetrical repetition of movement patterns is necessary in practice sessions for the dancer to develop maximum dexterity. In the context of dances, such symmetrical repetition is common but not mandatory.

Movement Characteristics: Use of Body Parts

Hands. Perhaps the feature most often associated with the dance of India is the highly articulated use of hand/finger positions. Although the hands are most fully exploited in expressive dance, they are also an integral part of pure dance.

The fingers are often extended so that they round slightly over the back-of-the-hand surface (see Figure 4)--a configuration described in the Western world as "hyper-extending." This emphasizes the length of the hand and extends the line of the arm outward.

While all of the fingers may be placed in a parallel fashion, it is more common that each finger has its own identity--each contributes to an overall shape of the hand, while having its own placement.

Additionally, each finger is not necessarily treated as a single entity. Often the hand is further segmented by isolating individual sections of a finger through articulating the joints within a finger (see, for example, the thumb and ring finger in Figure 4a).

Thus, the fingers are treated as highly individuated body parts, but at the same time contribute to a unified shape of the hand as a whole.

In expressive dance a large number of hand gestures are used to communicate the story or idea of the accompanying song text. In pure dance a very limited number of the same gestures is used, but they serve a strictly decorative function; they enhance the movement being executed by the rest of the body.

Feet. The primary function of the feet is to contribute to the rhythmic component of the dance. The dancer performs bare-footed, with several rows of bells fastened to her ankles (see, for example, Colorplate III). She stamps her feet in complex rhythmic patterns that sometimes coincide with those of the accompanying music, and sometimes create their own rhythmic counterpoint to that of the accompanying music (but correspond exactly with the rhythm performed by the *naṭṭuvanar*--see the section **Movement Characteristics: Use of Time**)--but her feet also occasionally remain silent to provide a kind of respite from the tension created by complex interrelated dancer and musician patterns.

Three surfaces of the foot make distinct contact with the ground. The most commonly used is the entire surface (as in the *taṭṭu aḍavu*). Rather than rolling through the foot to gradually bring its entire surface into contact with the ground, the dancer brusquely strikes it with the entire flat foot. Driving the heel into the ground or gradually rolling from the ball of the foot through to the heel will simply not produce the correct sound. The foot must be relaxed, with the force coming from the downward thrust of the leg. [8]

Sometimes the ball of the foot strikes the ground (as in some variants of the *naṭṭu aḍavu*--see, for example, Figure 6, count 5). When this happens, the ball of the foot striking the ground is generally placed close to the other foot--either alongside, in front of, or behind it--the non-striking foot remaining flat on the ground.

The final surface that makes contact with the ground is the heel. When this is done, the leg is usually extended to the side or the front, with the knee straight (as in the *naṭṭu aḍavu*--see, for example, Figure 7, counts 1 and 5). In order to accommodate the heel contact, the ankle is flexed at a right angle. Sometimes the leg is relaxed so that the heel is dropped to firmly strike the ground, causing the ankle bells to sound. This is different, however, from the leg driving the full foot into contact with the ground. At other times the heel is quietly placed on the ground so there is no stamp or sounding of the bells.

When the foot is lifted from the ground, it is either held in a relaxed position that simply extends the line of the lower leg, or the ankle is specifically flexed at a right angle. But the foot is never pointed, as in Western ballet.

Head. Movements of the head in pure dance function largely as the hands do--they enhance the movement of the body as a whole rather than serving as focal points. The side-to-side shifting of the head is undoubtedly the most widely-known movement. In performance, however, it is found relatively infrequently. One of its most important uses--and one of the rare instances when it is important as an isolated movement--is in an *alārippu*. At the beginning of an *alārippu* lateral movements of the head are performed in isolation in a variety of rhythmic patterns.[9]

Most frequently the head tilts and turns in order for the eyes to focus on one or both of the hands. A statement in the *Abhinayadarpaṇam* indicates

> Where the hand goes, there go the eyes.
> Where the eyes go, there goes the mind.
> Where the mind goes, there goes the *rasa* [aesthetic mood].

In expressive dance the facial focus on the hands helps draw attention to them as communicating body parts. In pure dance, the focus on the hands contributes to the overall shape of the movement.

Facial expression is of prime importance in expressive dance. In pure dance, it simply functions to enhance the overall movement pattern. Very occasionally--as in some sections of an *alārippu*--the focus of the eyes will shift quickly from side-to-side to enhance the sideward shifting of the head.

Torso. While the hands and fingers are highly articulated, the torso moves primarily as a single unit. The basic stance utilizes an upright torso, with pelvis and chest aligned. The torso occasionally tilts, but when it does, it tilts as a single unit--bending occurs at the hip joint, and not elsewhere in the spine. Tilts occur both to the side and to the front (see Figure 9, counts 1-2 and 5-6).

Occasionally the torso maintains its upright position, but twists (see Figure 7, count 5). This is generally done to enhance a leg gesture that is extended forward, or to allow the head to focus on a leg gesture that is extended backward.

The torso is most typically upright, with the arms and legs moving--in a kind of counterpoint--against a held (stationary) torso.

Legs. There are two major supporting positions assumed by the legs. When the knees are straight, the legs are parallel so the toes point directly forward; when the knees are bent, the legs are outwardly-rotated as much as possible, the ideal being the knees and toes pointing directly to the sides (see Figure 1). While the straight-knee position is sometimes used in pure dance, the bent-knee position predominates; the emphasis is clearly down, with the knees ideally bent at slightly more than a ninety-degree angle. An often-heard reprimand from teachers is "Sit down more!"

Use of the legs in pure dance is not extensive. They may gesture forward, sideward, or backward, but limit their sphere of movement largely to contact with the ground. They will occasionally be lifted in a bent-knee position with the foot near to the knee of the supporting leg, but do not make large, high gestures as is so frequently done in Western ballet. The legs function more to aid in the rhythmic stamping of the feet and to contribute to the overall flow of the movement, rather than as a primary focal point for movement intricacies.

Arms. Movements of the arms show the greatest variety in pure dance in Bharata Nāṭyam. They make large excursions through space, sometimes as a single unit (see Figure 11), and sometimes segment into upper arm, lower arm, hand, and fingers (see Figure 8, starting position). They change quickly from large movements of the entire arm to smaller units of one portion of the arm, and frequently assume angular, segmented positions (see Figure 6, counts 5-6).

Relationships Between Body Parts. During the course of a dance individual body parts move in different relationships to each other. Sometimes small movements of isolated body parts--particularly the hand, lower arm, and head--may occur. At other times large movements of large body parts--such as the whole arm--occur. And at still other times small or large movements of different body parts occur simultaneously.

Movement Characteristics: Use of Time

Time is a particularly important element in pure dance in Bharata Nāṭyam. In many respects, the dancer can be looked upon as a musician, contributing to the sound dimension with the stamping of her feet and the subsequent sounding of her ankle bells--in a sense visualizing the rhythmic component of the music. This is particularly noteworthy because in expressive dance she visualizes the meaning--or one of many meanings--of the song text.

It is the tight interplay between musicians and dancer (dancer-cum-musician) that creates much of the excitement in a Bharata Nāṭyam performance. At times, the rhythm sounded by the musicians is identical with that sounded and visually portrayed by the dancer. At other times, however, there is an underlying rhythmic structure to which musicians and dancer adhere, but each realizes it in a quite different way, seeming to wander off into his or her own realm. The audience is torn between the driving force of each, but a resolution comes for all when musicians, who function as one rhythmic unit, and dancer, who functions as another, conclude their phrases simultaneously on the metrical beat known as *sum*.[10]

One musician is a major exception to the frequent rhythmic variances between the dancer and accompanying musicians. The *naṭṭuvanar* (who is generally the dancer's teacher) plays a small pair of cymbals, and the rhythmic pattern he plays is always identical with that performed by the dancer.

A particularly interesting feature occurs in one portion of the performance. In a *varṇam* the dancer's upper body (torso, arms, hands, and face) is used to express the content of the sung text. The dancer's legs, however, are engaged in maintaining a ground-base--stamping out a fixed rhythmic pattern related to the *tāla* (underlying rhythmic structure) of the piece. These rhythmic stampings are known as *tatti mettu*. At the conclusion of the textual verse, the dancer executes a special rhythmic cadence to "finish off" the section. This is extremely difficult to perform because the dancer must concentrate on two very differnet kinds of activities, and is extremely exciting to watch, beacuse the viewer is strongly aware of both the rhythmic and textual dimensions performed by the dancer.

Variety in the use of time is also important. Within a single dance, while the musical accompaniment maintains a fixed rhythmic structure the same movement pattern may be repeated in one or more different rhythmic patterns and at several different speeds. Relationship to the music is achieved by inserting pauses, or condensing movements in time by "squeezing" them into fewer musical beats. If necessary, the dancer fills out the musical rhythmic cycle by repeating a movement pattern until the cycle is completed, or by adding a short movement pattern to the beginning of the phrase.

Another way in which variety is achieved in the use of time is by stringing together movement patterns of unequal lengths, so that when performed to a consistent underlying rhythmic accompaniment the accents in the movements (and hence, the sound created by stamping) continually shift with respect to the accents in the music.

Movement Characteristics: Use of Space

Overall Orientation. The dancer is primarily oriented to the front of the performing space. Turns are occasionally performed (see, for example, Figure 8, counts 3-4), but if a full turn is done it is performed quickly and the dancer immediately returns to her frontal orientation.

Emphasis on Poses. In contrast to dance in some traditions in which emphasis is placed on the flow of movement, and the audience is aware of a kind of on-goingness, Bharata Nāṭyam emphasizes poses.

> The sculpturesque quality of Indian dance does not need emphasis, but it must be understood that the pose or stance in the dance is all important. Indian dance is, in fact a stringing together of a number of highly stylized and symbolic poses. The *nritta* technique encompasses not only the technique of rendering rhythm (*tala*) through movements which do not have meaning, but also the important feature of projecting specific poses within a given rhythmic cycle.[11]

If it were not for the speed of many of the dance movements, it would be quite easy to take still photographs of Bharata Nāṭyam because of this emphasis on continually arriving at prescribed destinations.

It should be kept in mind that the notion of emphasis on poses is relative: obviously any dance form that carried this to an extreme would no longer be dance. While qualitative differences may be found in different styles of Bharata Nāṭyam, in comparison to such other traditional Indian forms as Manipuri and Mohiniāṭṭam, Bharata Nāṭyam emphasizes the poses in which movement phrases culminate rather than the flow of movement that leads to them.

Use of Space Surrounding the Dancer's Body. The dancer may be envisioned as occupying an imaginary bubble identified by Western movement analysts as the kinesphere. This bubble is bounded by all the surfaces the dancer could touch by extending her limbs in all direction, without transporting her body through space. The kinesphere is divided into three zones, depending on proximity to the dancer's body--near-, medium-, and far-reach space.

The Bharata Nāṭyam dancer makes full use of her kinesphere. Near-reach space is used by the arms for "resting" positions at the beginning or ending of a phrase (as in variant 3 of *naṭṭu aḍavu*--see Figure 8) or as a momentary transition between phrases (as in the last part of count 4 in variant 4 of *naṭṭu aḍavu*--see Figure 9). Near-reach space is also used by the legs in their narrow stance, to which they continually return in pure dance (see Figure 1).

Far-reach space is used extensively by the arms, which extend upward, downward, and in any direction. The legs, too, extend in all directions, but not at all levels--they gesture downward, and occasionally lift to break their contact with the ground, but *never* extend upward above the hips. A story is told of the god Śiva (The Lord of Dance) having a dance contest with the goddess Kālī. Śiva would execute a movement and then Kālī would attempt to duplicate it. The contest went on for some time until Śiva executed a movement in which he lifted his leg quite high. The contest ended immediately because Kālī refused to execute such a masculine gesture.

The story of Śiva's leg gesture and Kālī's refusal to perform it, and the absence of high leg gestures in Bharata Nāṭyam--traditionally a female dance genre--are interesting because of the numbers of dance sculptures on temples in which female figures are depicted with one leg in a high extension.

Progression Through Space. There is relatively little use of locomotion in pure dance. In some dances the performer remains in one spot for long periods of time and executes movement patterns that do not progress through space. (The basic motif and first four variants of the *naṭṭu aḍavu* group do not contain any locomotion.) This, and the predominant frontal orientation, may be related to the fact that Bharata Nāṭyam was originally performed in front of an image of a deity in a temple: space may simply have been limited, and it would have been inappropriate for the dancer to turn her back to the deity. In modern performance styles, however, dancers tend to make fuller use of turns and the performing space available to them.

Because of the emphasis on positions, most pure dance movement in Bharata Nāṭyam displays a clear sense of directness. The dancer projects an image of shooting directly for poses, rather than meandering and gradually arriving at a destination. Because of this, also, many movements emphasize a straight-line path from one position to the next, with the audience frequently not being aware of how the dancer moved from one pose to the next. Often movements have a "poking" or "thrusting" quality, such as arm gestures that begin tucked in close to the torso and then thrust forward in a straight line to arrive in a fully extended position (see Figure 9, counts 4-5).

Circular movements occasionally occur, but are most frequently executed by the arms. (This may be seen in variants 5 and 6 of the *naṭṭu aḍavu*--Figures 10 and 11.)

Overall there is a flat, planar quality to the pure dance of Bharata Nāṭyam, with the greatest emphasis on the lateral, or side-to-side plane. Circular movements occur *within* a plane, but seldom cut across from one plane to another.

Angularity. While curved movements and positions occur, there is an emphasis on angularity in pure dance, with the triangle being the predominant shape (see Figure 3).

> The line joining the two shoulders may be conceived as the base of one triangle and the waist as the imaginary apex of an inverted triangle. From this apex a second triangle is conceived with the thighs as the two sides and the line joining the two knees as the base of this triangle. The third triangle is formed by the space covered by the two calves and the line joining the two knees. The arms reinforce this by forming other triangles on either side--the extended arm forming one side of the triangle and the line joining the hand to the knee suggesting the second.[12]

Relationship to Gravity. Although there is a sense of verticality in pure dance because of the predominantly upright torso, there is also a sense of groundedness. The emphasis on the bent-knee position, the stamps driving downward into the gound, the absence of high leg extensions and emphasis on the feet contacting the floor, and the emphasis on landing and de-emphasis on height during the only occasional jumps, all contribute to an earthy quality. But the vertical torso and expansive use of the arms prevent this connection with the ground from becoming heavy.

Movement Characteristics: Use of Energy

As with many dance forms, the dancer's movements should appear effortless. At the same time, however, the Bharata Nāṭyam dancer projects the illusion of a tremendously high energy level.

This energy level seems to come from five elements: the speed with which movements are executed, the density of movement,[13] the driving, percussive nature of the intricate rhythmic patterns stamped out with the feet, the tension created between dance rhythm and music rhythm, and the occasional tension created by the concurrent use of differing qualities in different parts of the dancer's body.

While fluidity is present in many movements (such as the large, flowing arm-circle in variant 6 of *naṭṭu aḍavu*--see Figure 11), the predominant quality is sharp and staccato. At times, (such as when a ground-base is being stamped out with the feet while the upper body is executing expressive dance, as described earlier in the *varṇam*), the dancer performs two differing qualities concurrently--a combination that produces a very dynamic performance.

Summary

The pure dance of Bharata Nāṭyam is a study in contrasts, contrasts in the use of body parts, time, space, and energy. And it is these contrasts that create excitement and diversity in performance. While expressive dance requires an informed audience--an audience knowledgeable of the traditional literature and symbolic code of movement--pure dance can be appreciated by even the uninformed. Although based on a complex theory of movement, the purpose of pure dance is simply to display the beauty of the body in motion--a kind of motion that comes about through an intricate interplay of movement and stillness that is distinctive to Bharata Nāṭyam.

> The Western dancer is reaching out into space vertically and horizontally in order to arrest a moment of perfect dynamic movement. Whatever perfection the Western dancer achieves, he does by making geometrical patterns in space, where movement is conceived as an attempt to be free from gravity. The Indian dancer, on the other hand, attempts quite the opposite; consequently the two differ completely in their approach to movement. The Indian dancer's preoccupation is not so much with space as with time, with the dancer constantly trying to achieve the perfect pose to convey a sense of timelessness. The human form here achieves geometrical shapes in time rather than in space, for the intricacy of the *nritta* technique depends on the very fine and elaborate manipulation of rhythm (*tala*) to achieve a series of poses. The perfect pose is a moment of arrested time--in limited space.[14]

Figure 1
Taṭṭu Aḍavu: Starting Position

Plate 1. *Pārvatī (Śivakāmasundarī)*, early 11th century. Tanjore Art Gallery. Photo: George Kliger.

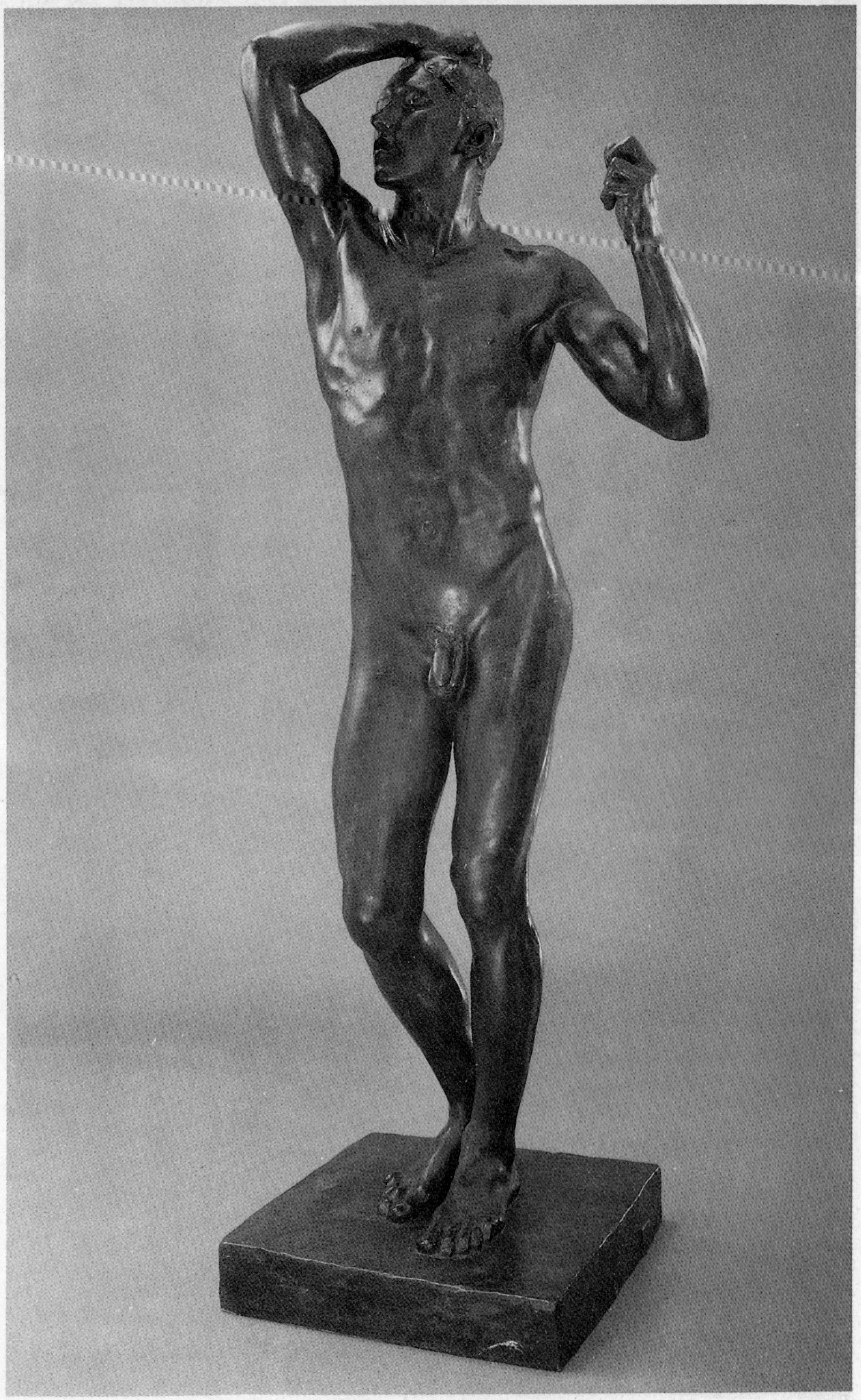

Plate 2. *Age of Bronze,* Auguste Rodin, 1875-77.
Photo: courtesy Minneapolis Institute of Arts.

Plate 3. *Naṭarāja* (from Kilayūr), 11th century. Tanjore Art Gallery.
Photo: George Kliger

Plate 4. *Naṭarāja*, mid-6th century. Cave I, Bādāmi.
Photo: Carol Bolon.

Plate 5. *Naṭarāja*, mid-6th century. Cave temple, Śiyamaṅgalam. Photo: Michael Rabe.

Plate 6. *Viṣṇu Trivikrama*, mid-7th century. Varāha Cave, Mahābalipuram. Photo: Michael Rabe.

Plate 7. *Gopuram, karaṇa* reliefs, 14th century. Naṭarāja temple, Cidambaram. Photo: George Kliger.

Plate 8. *Gopuram, karaṇa* reliefs, 14th century. Naṭarāja temple, Cidambaram. Photo: George Kliger.

Plate 9. Alarmel Valli in the spouse-goddess pose.
Photo: Thomas Foley.

Plate 10. Alarmel Valli in *Bhujaṅgatrāsita,* Naṭarāja pose.
Photo: Thomas Foley.

Plate 11. Alarmel Valli in *Talapuṣpapuṭa karaṇa*.
Photo: Thomas Foley.

Plate 12. Alarmel Valli in *Gajakrīḍita karaṇa*.
Photo: Thomas Foley.

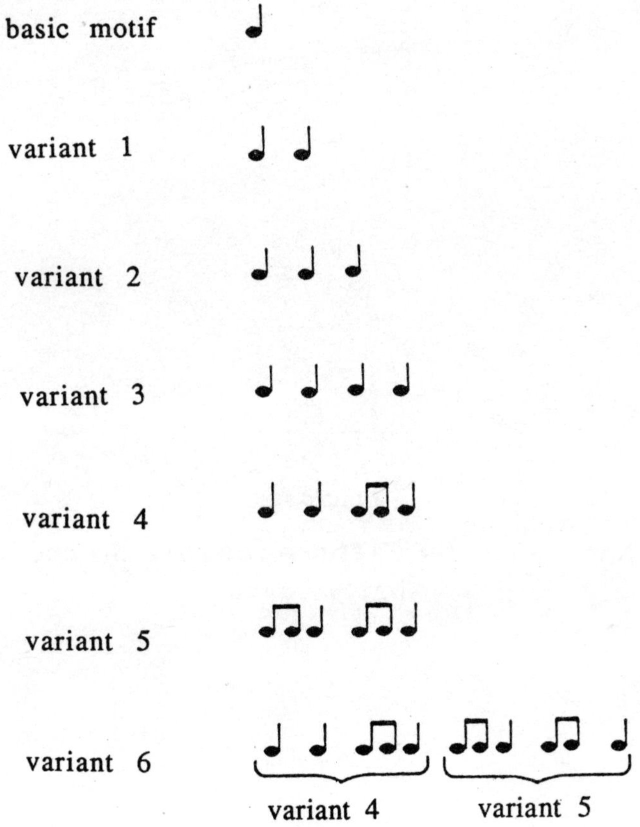

Figure 2

Taṭṭu Aḍavu: Rhythmic Patterns of Basic Motif and Variants

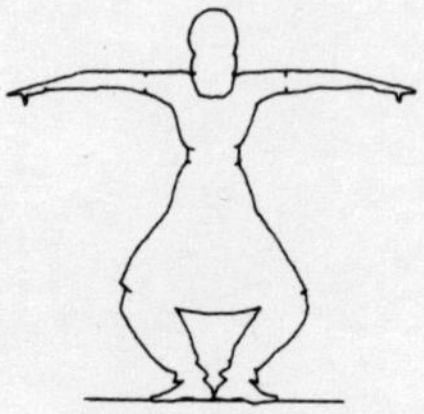

Figure 3

Alternate Arm Position for *Taṭṭu Aḍavu* and Starting Position for *Naṭṭu Aḍavu*

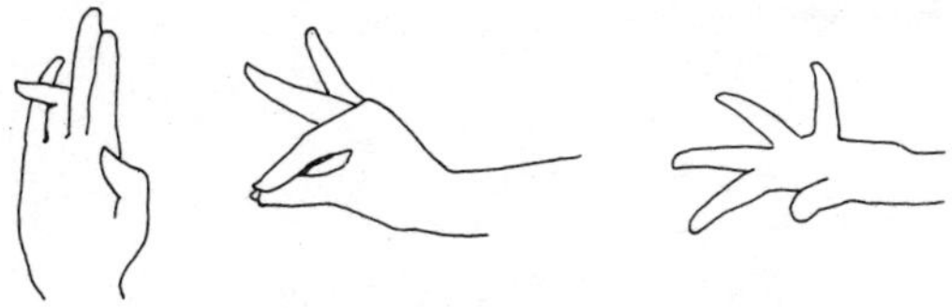

a *tripatāka* b *haṃsāsya* c *alapadma*

Figure 4
Hastas

Figure 5

Naṭṭu Aḍavu: Basic Motif

(It is impossible to fully represent movement in static illustrations. The sequences depicted in the figures are only intended to suggest the general nature of the flow of motion so that the reader may better understand the verbal descriptions in the text.)

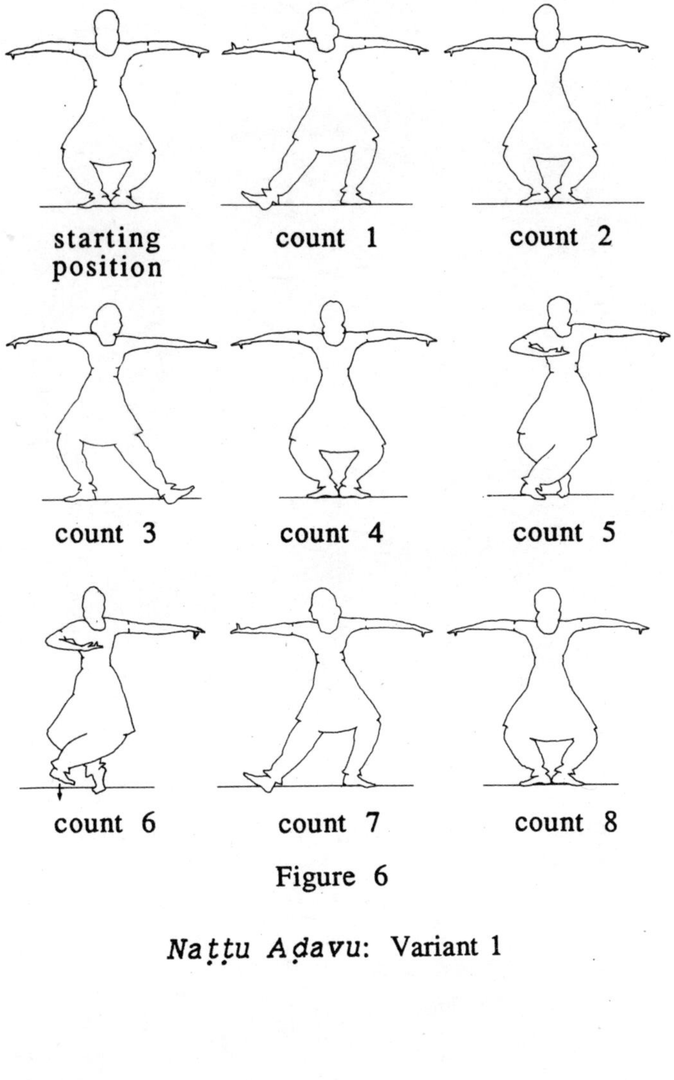

Figure 6

Naṭṭu Aḍavu: Variant 1

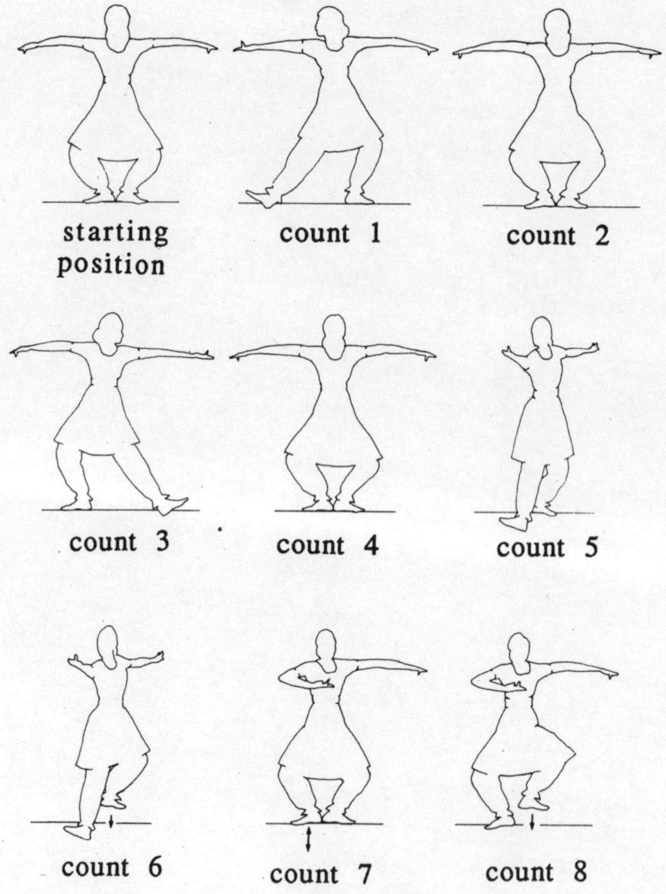

Figure 7

Naṭṭu Aḍavu: Variant 2

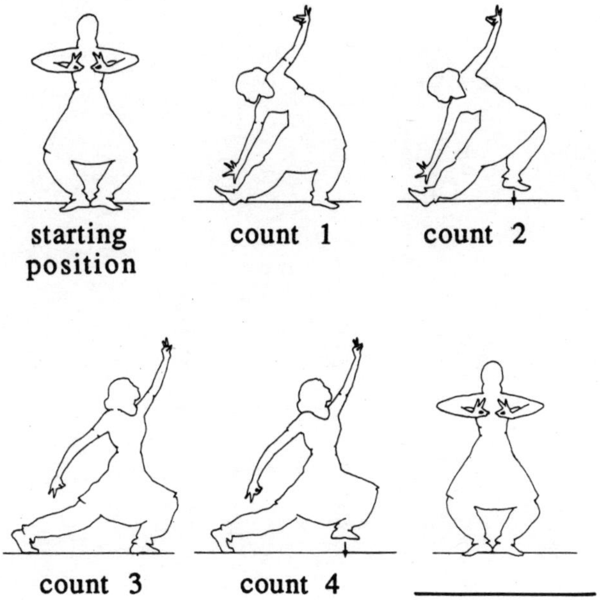

Figure 8

Naṭṭu Aḍavu: Variant 3

Figure 9

Naṭṭu Aḍavu: Variant 4

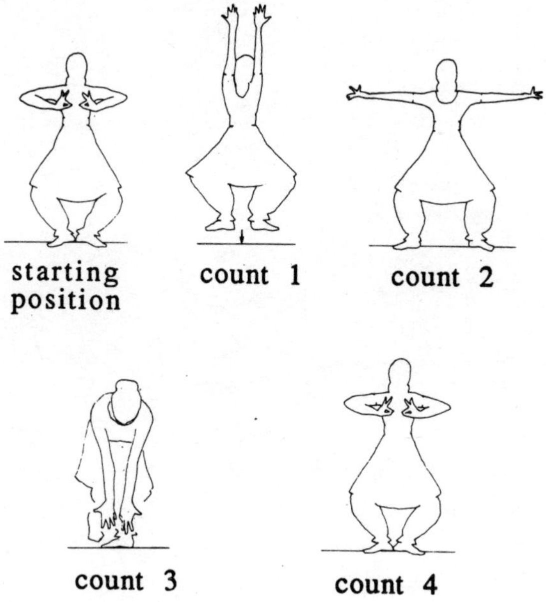

Figure 10

Naṭṭu Aḍavu: Variant 5

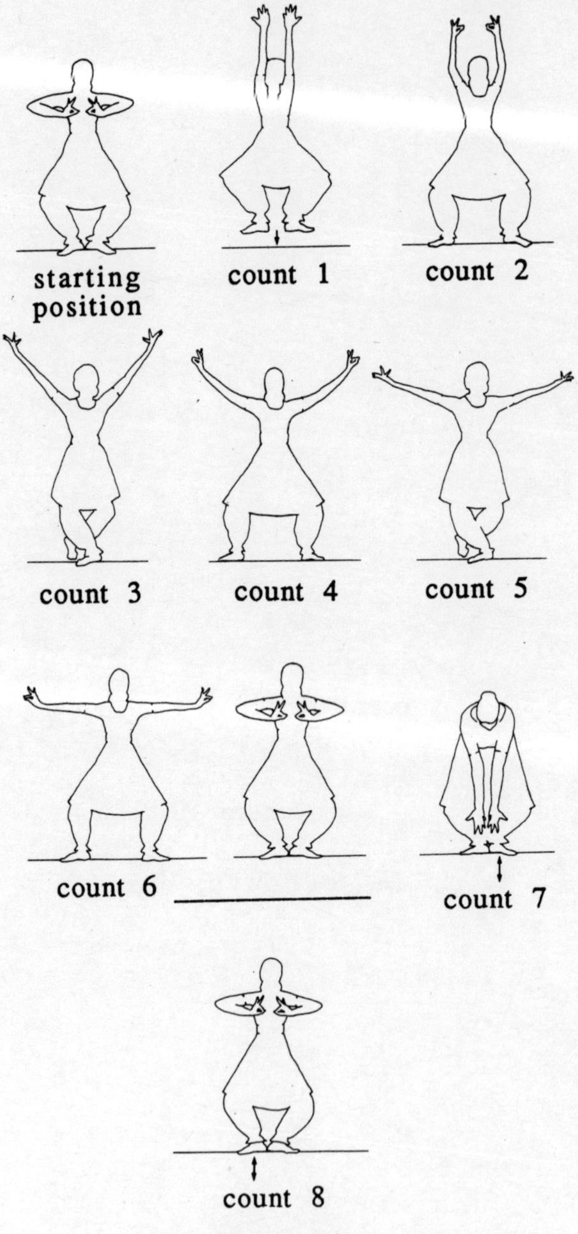

Figure 11

Naṭṭu Aḍavu: Variant 6

APPENDIX

Labanotation Scores of *Naṭṭu Aḍavu*

(Labanotation and autography by Judy Van Zile. The Labanotation has been checked by Jane Marriett, approved, and meets the qualifications for Labanotation scores set forth by the Dance Notation Bureau. It follows practices approved by the International Council for Kinetography Laban as of 1986. Because of the versatility of Labanotation, the scores that follow contain a greater amount of detail and accuracy than the preceding verbal descriptions and illustrations.)

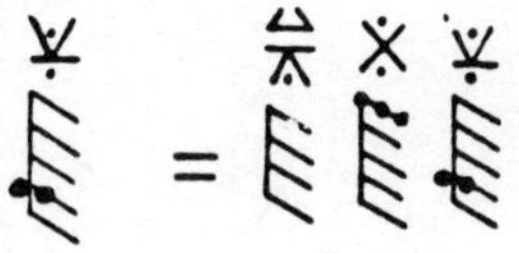

tripatāka hasta

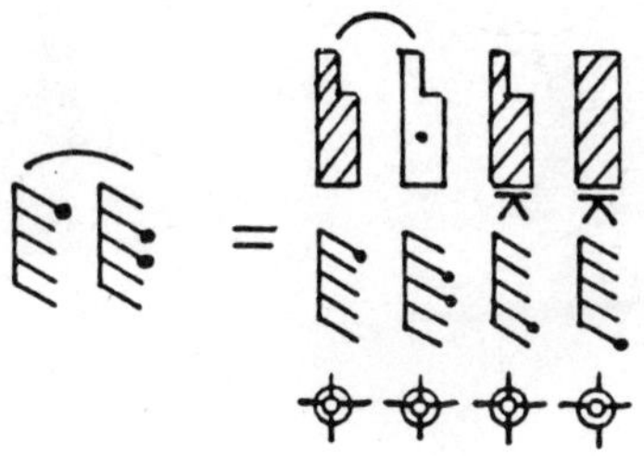

haṃsāsya hasta

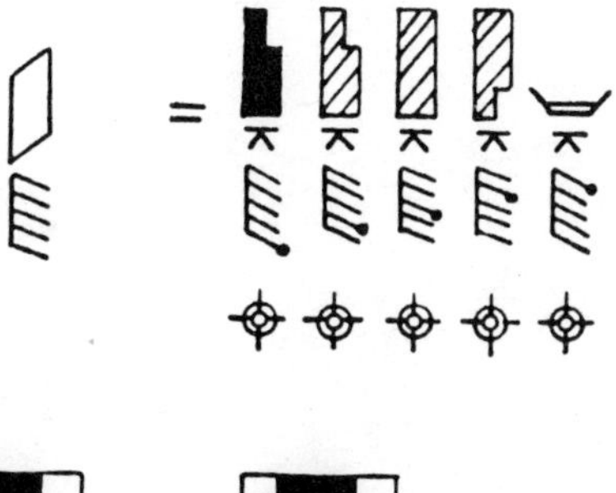

alapadma hasta

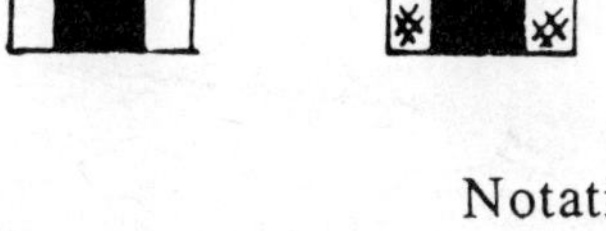

Notation Glossary

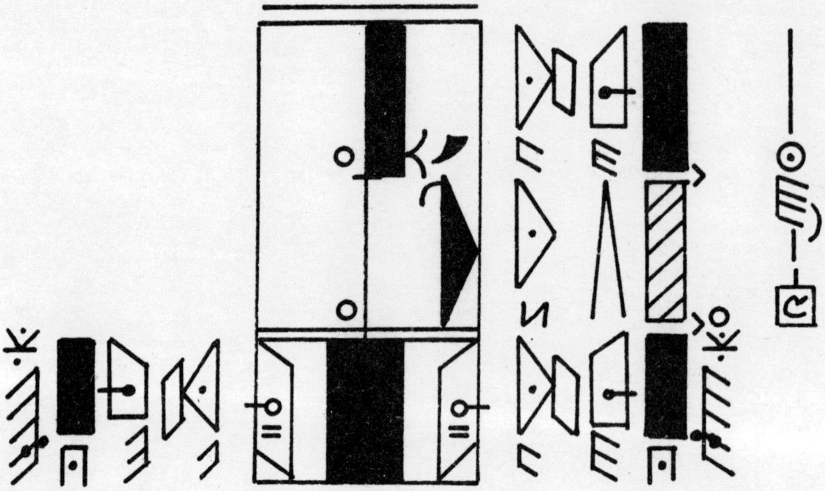

Basic Motif

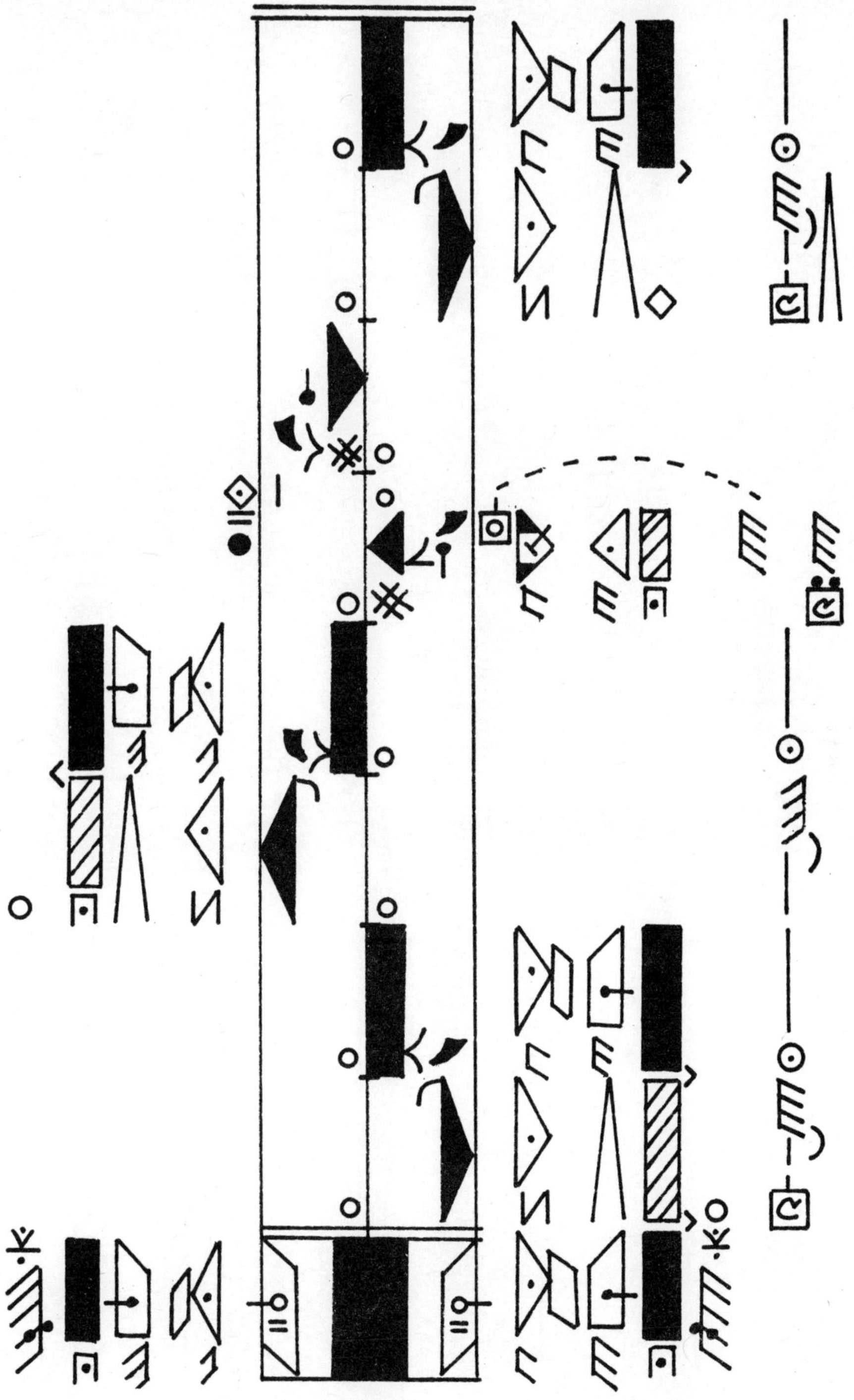

Variant 1

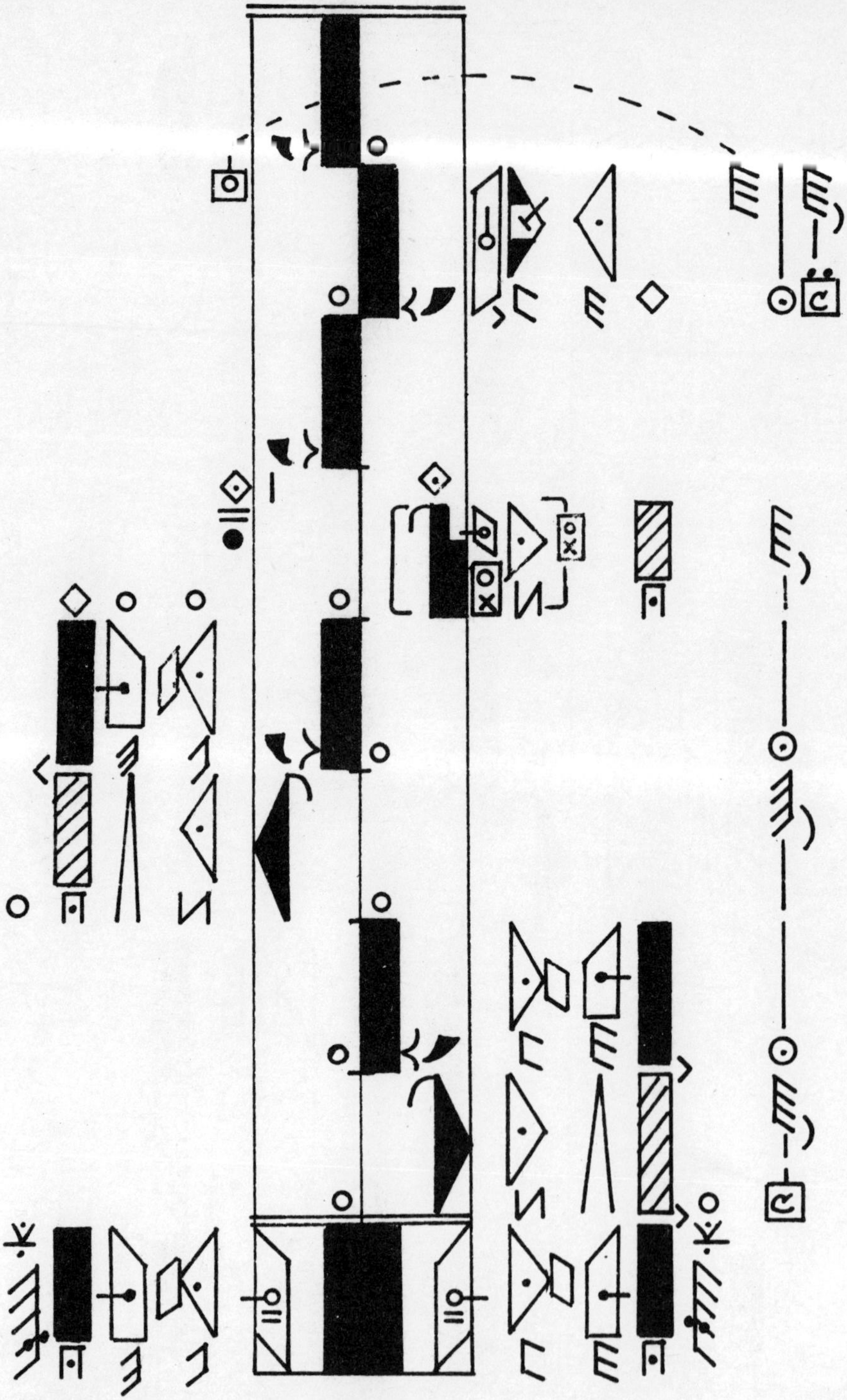

Variant 2

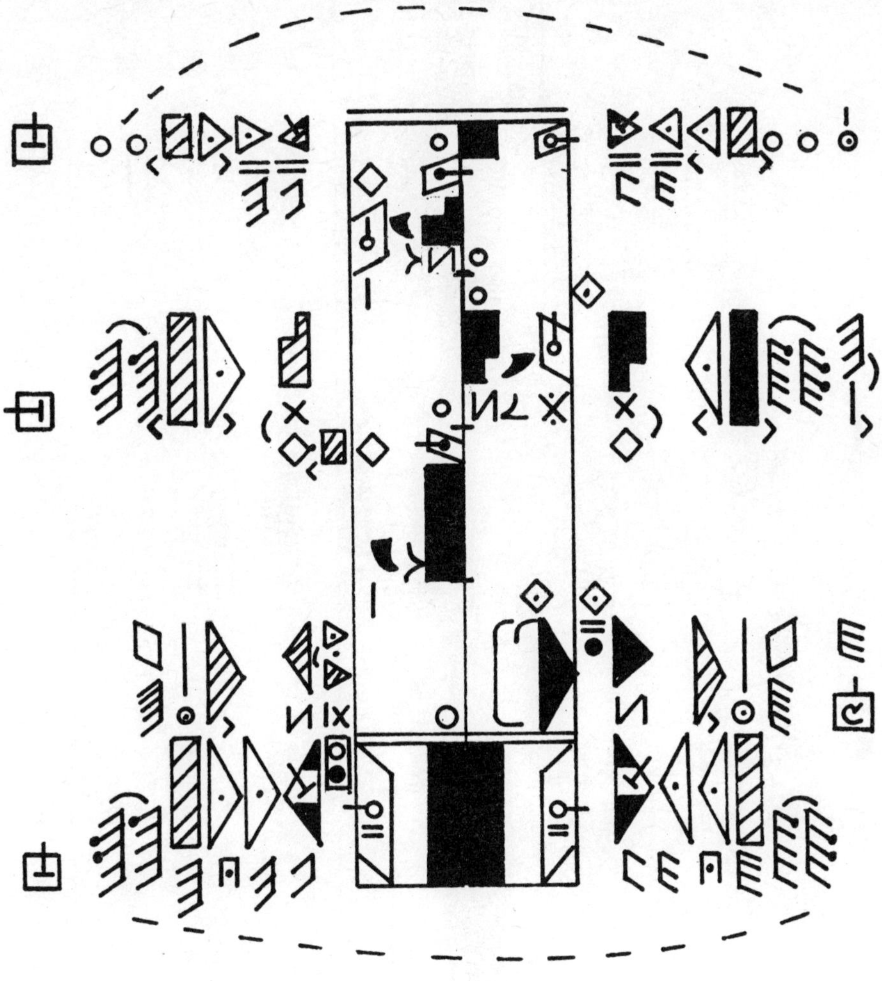

Variant 3

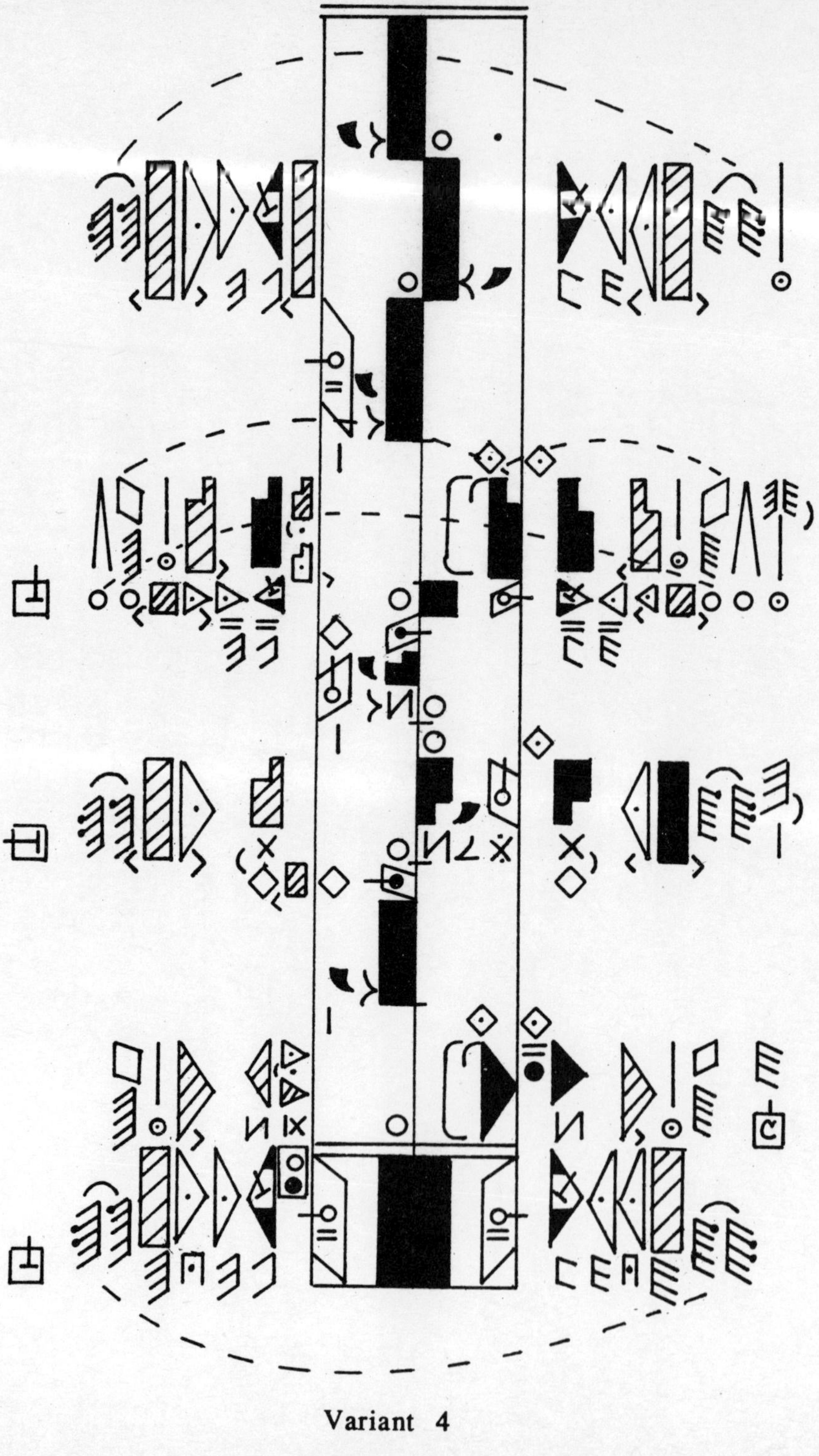

Variant 4

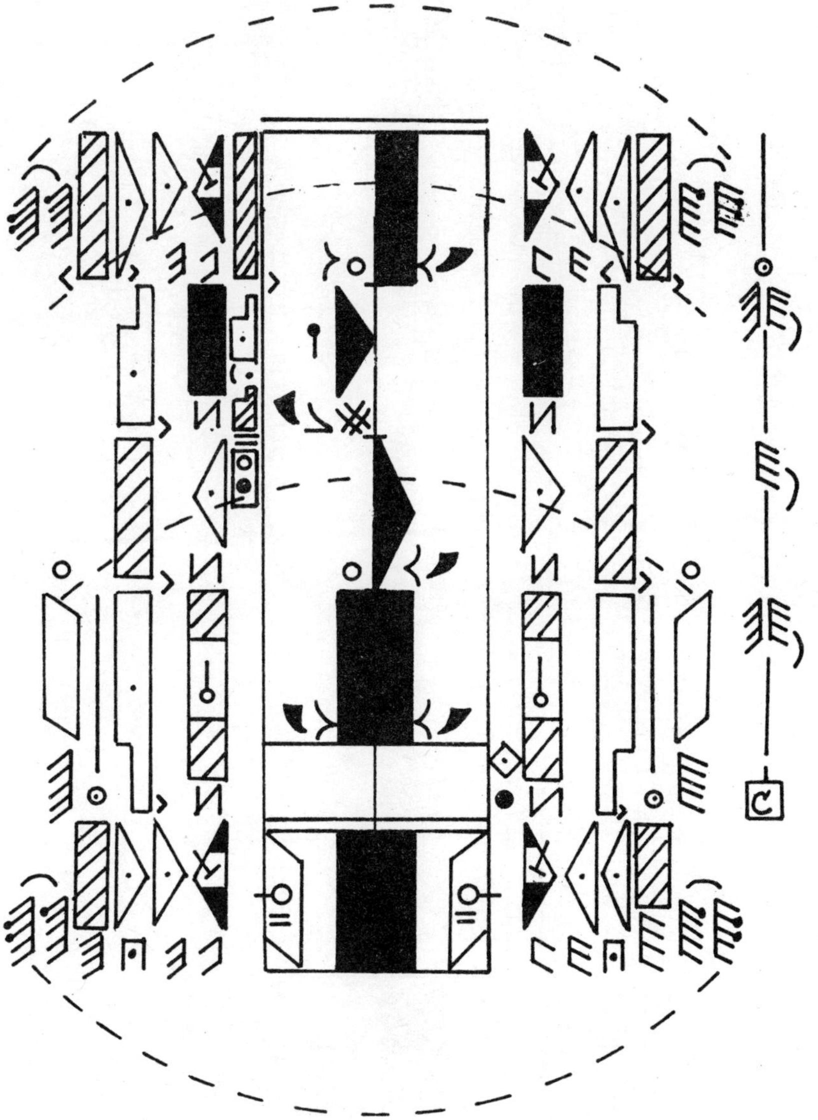

Variant 5

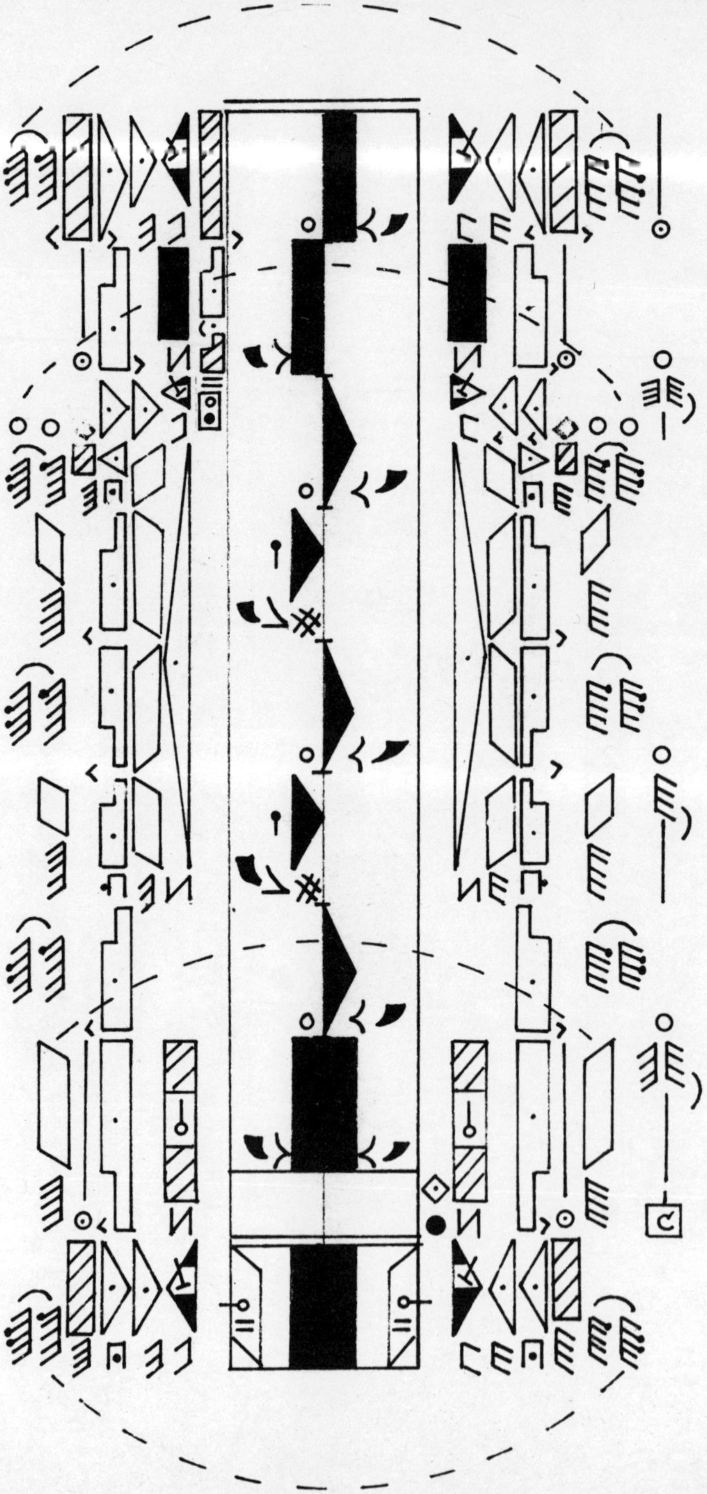

Variant 6

Notes

1. The author wishes to express appreciation to Betty True Jones, Barbara B. Smith, and Ricardo Trimillos for their helpful comments on an earlier version of this article; the University of Hawaii Center for Asian and Pacific Studies for funding assistance that enabled some of the illustrative materials; and a Fulbright grant that made the author's study of Bharata Nāṭyam in India possible. Appreciation is also expressed to Suzanne Stough for providing illustrations. The author is solely responsible for the content of the article.

2. The terms *hasta* and *mudrā* are frequently used interchangeably. Scholars often use the term *hasta* simply to refer to a position of the hand and fingers, and *mudrā* to refer to a position of the hand and fingers that has specific meaning--as in expressive dance. Because this article is concerned with pure dance, the term *hasta* is used (except in direct quotations, where the term used in the original source is retained).

3. Vatsyayan, Kapila, *Indian Classical Dance*, (New Delhi: Publications Divsion, Ministry of Information and Broadcasting, Government of India, 1974), p. 106.

4. Bharata Muni, *The Nāṭyaśāstra*, edited and translated by Manomohan Ghosh, 2nd rev. ed., vol. I (Calcutta: Manisha Granthalaya Private Limited, 1967); vol. II (Calcutta: Asiatic Society, 1961), IV: 66-68.

5. *Nāṭyaśāstra*, IV: 30-34.

6. Van Zile, Judy, "Balasaraswati's 'Tisram Alarippu': A Choreographic Analysis," in Bonnie C. Wade, ed., *Performing Arts in India: Essays of Music, Dance, and Drama* (Maryland: University Press of America. Monograph Series No. 21, Center for South and Southeast Asia Studies, University of California, Berkeley, 1982), pp. 47-104.

7. The author studied with Balasaraswati during the summer of 1967 at the American Society for Eastern Arts, Berkeley, California; during the summer of 1969 at the University of California, Los Angeles; and for 10 months, 1969-1970, in India.

8. Bartenieff, Irmgard, Peggy Hackney, Betty True Jones, Judy Van Zile, and Carl Wolz, "The Potential of Movement Analysis as a Research Tool: A Preliminary Analysis," *Dance Research Journal*, vol. 16, No. 1 (Spring, 1984), pp. 3-26.

9. Van Zile, "Balasaraswati's 'Tisram Alarippu': A Choreographic Analysis," pp. 79-83.

10. Higgins, Jon B., "Balasaraswati's 'Tisram Alarippu': The Musical Content," in Bonnie C. Wade, ed., *Performing Arts in India: Essays of Music, Dance, and Drama* (Maryland: University Press of America. Monograph Series No. 21, Center for South and Southeast Asia Studies, University of California, Berkeley, 1982), pp. 105-119, esp. p. 114.

11. Vatsyayan, *Indian Classical Dance*, p. 8.

12. Ibid., p. 17.

13. Van Zile, "Balasaraswati's 'Tisram Alarippu': A Choreographic Analysis," p. 64.

14. Vatsyayan, *Indian Classical Dance*, p. 9.

Bibliography

Bartenieff, Irmgard, Peggy Hackney, Betty True Jones, Judy Van Zile, and Carl Wolz, "The Potential of Movement Analysis as a Research Tool: A Preliminary Analysis," *Dance Research Journal*, Vol. 16, No. 1 (Spring, 1984), pp. 3-26.

Bharata Muni, *The Nāṭyaśāstra*, edited and translated by Manomohan Ghosh, 2nd rev. ed., vol. I (Calcutta: Manisha Granthalaya Private Limited, 1967); vol. II (Calcutta: Asiatic Society, 1961).

Higgins, Jon B, "Balasaraswati's 'Tisram Alarippu': The Musical Content," in Bonnie C. Wade, ed., *Performing Arts in India: Essays of Music, Dance, and Drama* (Maryland: University Press of America. Monograph Series No. 21, Center for South and Southeast Asia Studies, University of California, Berkeley, 1982), pp. 105-119.

Van Zile, Judy, "Balasaraswati's 'Tisram Alarippu': A Choreographic Analysis," in Bonnie C. Wade, ed., *Performing Arts in India: Essays of Music, Dance, and Drama* (Maryland: University Press of America. Monograph Series No. 21, Center for South and Southeast Asia Studies, University of California, Berkeley,1982), pp. 47-104

Vatsyayan, Kapila, *Indian Classical Dance* (New Delhi: Publications Division, Ministry of Information and Broadcasting, Government of India, 1974).

Vatsyayan, Kapila, *Classical Indian Dance in Literature and the Arts* (New Delhi: Sangeet Natak Akademi, 1968).

IV

Musical Dynamics In Bharata Nāṭyam: Freedom, Constraint and Devotion

Alan L. Kagan

To the Memory of Jon B. Higgins*

The consideration of music in dance genres is rarely given the attention it receives in a purely concert performance environment. This is unfortunate because the association with dance brings to music an additional set of meanings and intentions which are not otherwise present. Furthermore, in the situation of Bharata Nāṭyam the compositions must be understood as genres which are distinct from the autonomy of concert music in both form and content. The role of music as a servant of dance may place some special restraints upon the performers, but the musical product need not be viewed as an art lesser in status to that of the concert program when virtuosity is given full rein, often to the detriment of content.

The musicians of the dance ensemble comprise at least one vocalist, a *mṛdaṅgam* player (the major double-headed barrel-shaped drum of South India), a melody instrumentalist usually performing *vīṇā*, flute or violin, and the ubiquitous drone instrument, either a *tānpura* or the frequently encountered electronic "*śruti* box." To this standard concert medium must be added the *naṭṭuvanar*, usually a dance-master who plays small bronze cymbals, *tāḷam*, and who recites rhythmically dance syllables, *solluka.ṭ.ṭu*. Finally, one should acknowledge the dancer as percussionist, adding the timbres of ankle-bells and foot stamping to the aural medium. Furthermore, the dancer also has the option of singing during the dance, as Balasaraswati would do, yet Higgins observed that few "feel confident enough as musicians to attempt this."[1]

The construction of a Bharata Nāṭyam dance program is a standardized sequence of distinctive compositions which either focus on abstract dance (*nṛtta*), on interpretive dance (*nṛtya*) which is governed by the expressive arts of mime and gesture (*abhinaya*), or combine the two. On the musical side the needs of *nṛtta* are an emphasis on rhythmic articulation and mathematical complexity with simple melodic accompaniment, while for *nṛtya* it is varieties of expressive lyricism and subtle improvisation of melodic interpretation to support the individual phrases of text (*sāhitya*) and dance gestures. The sequence of genres progresses systematically in introducing each characteristic of dance and music with respect to *nṛtta* and *nṛtya*, then fusing the two for the psychological and technical high point of the program, the *pada varṇam*. After an intermission the performance proceeds through a set of compositions to gradually release the psychological tension. This moves from *abhinaya* themes of religious devotion (*bhakti*) and eroticism to light-hearted romance, then shifts back to the pure virtuoso display of abstract dance and its focus on rhythmic complexity. The performance ends, as it begins, with a presentation of homage to a deity.

A metric foundation, *tāla*, is essential for dance compositions with but one exception. The *śloka*, a devotional composition which concludes the performance, may be presented entirely without this pulse organization, and so it is devoid of metric and rhythmic patters, as well as percussion. It is now becoming a practice to open the program with a dedicatory *śloka*. For the rest of the program each composition opens in the same manner with an *ālāpana*, a freely-expressed non-metric improvisation of the modal and melodic character of that piece's *rāga* This, however, precedes the dance itself.

The selection of *rāgas* for Bharata Nāṭyam is both more and less restrictive than it is for music concerts. The dictum that a *rāga* should not be repeated within a concert does not hold for the dance performance. Rather, the concern for appropriateness of *rasa*, aesthetic mood, is a strong governing factor in *rāga* selectivity for the dance and overrides the concern regarding repetition. On the other hand, this dance emphasis on *rasa* generally precludes the use of those *rāgas* with moods inappropriate for the standard dance themes, or those regarded as demanding of the intellect rather than emotion. Lastly, the use of *rāgamālikā*, a "garland" or series of *rāgas*, is more commonly applied to dance compositions than to non-dance concert works and may be encountered more than once in the performance. *Rāgmālikā* provides more than a musical design for melodic variety. For devotional pieces in praise of deities or patron-rulers it produces a musical analogy for different personalities. *Rāgamālikā* can exhibit different aspects of *bhakti* within a single *rasa* as well as contrasting *rasas*. Spiritual devotion is expressed in many forms and characteristics, often displayed through metaphors which depict varieties of experience ranging from calm detachment to passionate emotion. As the system of *rasas* is a classification of moods, this metaphorical linkage permits the embedding of *rasas* in *bhakti*. Similarly, the association of *rasas* with *rāgas* provides a means of using a sequence of *rāgas* to suggest either subtle varieties of one mood or the conflicting attributes of different *rasas*. For example, the various expressions of *karuṇa rasa* (pathos) can be suggested by the distinctions between *rāgas Śahāna* and *Punnāgavarāḷi*, while these contrast strongly with the romantic mood (*śṛṅgāra rasa*) of *rāga Khamās*.

The contemporary arrangement of a Bharata Nāṭyam program is not known to have existed before the nineteenth century, and this is equally true for many of the specific dance and musical characteristics of individual genres. The present format appears to have been the contribution of four brothers who excelled in the arts of dance, music and poetry. All born in the first decade of the nineteenth century, they were hereditary *naṭṭuvanars* of the Bṛhadīśvara temple in Tanjore, trained in music by Muthuswāmi Dīkṣitar, one of the most renowned of Carnatic composer-poets, and attached to the Tanjore court of Mahārāja Serfoji II. Best known as The Tanjore Quartette, they were all dance teachers. Each had individual prominence: Chinniah as dancer and teacher, Ponniah as composer-poet, Śivanandam as composer and *vīṇā* performer, and Vaḍivelu as composer and violinist.[2] The program sequence devised under their direction has remained fixed to this day with only minor changes.[3]

Alārippu. The standard opening, an abstract dance to display body movements and counter-rhythms of dance against the unvarying percussion pattern, is titled *alārippu*. The *naṭṭuvanar* chants a *sollukaṭṭu* text, a fixed system of dance mnemonics derived from drum vocalizations. These are a vocabulary of syllables created for dance instruction but which have been organized into artistically devised patterns, just as *mṛdaṅgam* players have done. They provide a suitable vocalization medium for *nṛtta* portions of dance. A secondary function of *alārippu* has become that of an invocation. Originally preceding the dance, a hymn is now sung during the dance. The two remain disparate in the sense that there is no connective relationship between the dance movements and the devotional text with its melody. Of course, this melody must conform to the conventional metric patterns used for this dance, a choice of three-, five-, seven-, or nine-pulse units, and the text of the hymn is arranged to adhere to the predetermined dance sectionalization.

Higgins commented on the lack of musical demands made on the part of the singer and melody instrumentalist.[4] However, the simultaneity of chanted *sollukaṭṭu* with the melodic rendition of the devotional text produces a polyphonic texture which is unique and not encountered elsewhere in dance or music concerts. This textural complexity replaces the conventional norm for "difficulty."

The standard hymn texts are in praise of Lord Subrahmaṇya, son of Śiva, and are sung in Tamil. Since the Hindu pantheon contains many deities and a multiplicity of deity names, one often encounters interchangeability. This may occur as alternative designations for one deity, as discrete entities associated with a central supreme figure-- such as the incarnations of Viṣṇu--or as gods of different regional and historic origin who have come to be considered equivalents. For example, the *alārippu* hymn used by the dancer Alarmel Valli was dedicated to Murugan, the Dravidian god of both war and beauty, whose alter identity is Subrahmaṇya. The *rāga* used was *Nāṭakurañji*.[5]

Jatisvaram. The second dance item continues the theme of *nṛtta*--the portrayal of "pure" movement--with increased complexity. The "text" is an alternation of *sollukaṭṭu* and *svara* (melodic solfege performed by the vocalist) in sections producing a rondo structure. The content of music and choreography being fixed in advance, there is little improvisation for the musicians. Dance genres with no *sāhitya* (text) are simply identified by the *rāga* selected and the composer of the melodic and rhythmic content. Some prominent composers of *jatisvaram* have been Veena Kuppaier of the eighteenth century, Vaḍivelu of the nineteenth century's Tanjore Quartette and K. Ponniah Pillai of the twentieth century.

Śabdam. The next dance item in the program shifts the focus to textual interpretation, *abhinaya*. *Śabdam*, meaning "praise," is based on a brief poem of four lines in praise of a deity or patron. This textual simplicity is used to organize the musical performance in four sections. The musical emphasis is grounded in lyrical expression rather than the rhythmic concerns of the preceding dances, yet carried out at a brisk tempo. Specific constraints for *tāla* and *rāga* are placed on the performers as the meter is always done in the seven-pulse organization of *miśra cāpu* and the *rāga* fixed to *Kāmbhōji*. Yet, this *rāga* limitation can be relaxed by the permitted use of a *rāga* garland which would begin with *Kāmbhōji*.

Higgins' analysis of a Balasaraswati's *śabdam* performance illustrates the significant degree of freedom in *rāga* choice within this *rāgamālikā* constraint.[6] The composition *Sarasijākṣulu* was created by the Tanjore brother Vaḍivelu. The *rāgas* specified for the first and fourth lines with their respective dance sections are *Kāmbhōji* and *Suraṭi*. The middle two lines are sung to any of a variety of *rāgas*, but Balasaraswati preferred to use *Bhairavī* followed by *Nāṭakurañji*. Except for *Bhairavī*, all three of the other *rāgas* belong to the same *mēḷa*, a "parent" pitch-set classification. It would be most interesting to clarify the role Vaḍivelu had in establishing this freedom of *rāga* choice for his text, since it also presumes a freedom of melodic creativity for future performers.

Śabdam does not always receive a favorable rating from connoisseurs and performers. The economy in its text places limits on the variety of expression one can utilize. Similarly, the fast tempo restricts the duration of each line and the expansion of mood which is more readily produced at a leisurely pace. Higgins wrote of the artistic difficulty required of both singer and dancer in maintaining interest through so many short repetitions and the need for subtle devices of variation.[7] He observed that a *śabdam's* "single most important stylistic feature . . . is that combination of poetic articulation and melodic phrasing which creates an interesting yet unobtrusive flow of musical-poetic imagery."[8]

Pada Varṇam. The first half of the program concludes with a composition testing the full range of the dancer's abilities. The *pada varṇam* is the longest of all Bharata Nāṭyam dance items, lasting up to an hour or more. Alternatively, a *svarajati* may be performed.

These are works complex in several ways, combining all aspects of dance, both abstract and interpretive, having a long and emotionally varied text with interpolations of *sollukaṭṭu* and *svaras*, providing a great variety of techniques for the musicians and having an intricate structural design. This design comprises four sections. The first is the *rāga ālāpana* preceding the entrance of the dancer. It is longer than the introductory *rāga* explorations used for the other types of compositions in Bharata Nāṭyam, giving immediate and continuous attention to the melody performers who may alternate between vocalist and instrumentalist, as is done in concerts.

The opening dance section is an interpretation of two couplets, the *pallavi* and *anupallavi*. Each textual line forms a subsection. They are separated from each other by other subsections of particularly complex rhythmic phrases chanted with *sollukaṭṭu*, the *tirmānam*. Thus, the dancer alternates abstract movements with expressive mime and the musicians are similarly alternating a focus on a mathematical rhythmic identity with a careful portrayal of text content paralleling the dancer's *abhinaya* gestures. The linguistically knowledgeable audience becomes aware that "a certain amount of 'word-painting' is in evidence" as musicians seek means to depict the text through musical representations of material objects, actions, events and emotions.[9] The audience should observe how carefully the musicians follow the dancer's lead in these *abhinaya* sections. Improvisation of melodic phrase and rhythmic pattern takes on a special meaning when the musicians are led by the decisions of a non-musician, the dancer, who can emphasize a word by extending the duration of the gesture.

The third section, *muktāyi svara*, is a four-line verse preceded and followed by the singing of *svaras* and closing with the opening line of the *pallavi* text. Finally, the last texted dance section, the *caraṇa*, comprises a one-line refrain which alternates in rondo fashion with a series of couplets: poetic images shifting from the erotic to the spiritual and providing a concentration on the depiction of emotional and dramatic experiences. Before the final *caraṇa* refrain the imagery is relieved with a subsection of *svara* singing.

For an analysis of a specific *pada varṇam* performance I will describe the contents of *Sami ninné kōri nānura* by the Tanjore Quartette brother Ponniah, as performed by Alarmel Valli's troupe at their 1986 concert at the University of Minnesota.[10] The text is in Telugu and is concerned with a devotee's appeal to Lord Śiva. The *tāla* is *rūpakam*, a metric grouping of six pulses in a pattern of two plus four. The *rāga* determination is the organization of a *rāgamālikā*, rather than a single *rāga* for the entire composition. This provides for yet another level of complexity in the intricate structure, while giving a clearer definition to the design of the performance, since each change of *rāga* coincides with a line of text.

In this text the heroine expresses devotion to Śiva, whom she perceives as her protector, whose love is overwhelming and whom she anxiously desires.

Pallavi: (1) Sami ninné kōri nānura[11]
Lord, I think only of you, endlessly.
(2) Sada nivu nennélu kōrā
Protect me forever.

Anupallavi: (1) Prema miraga Tanja puri vāsa
I am filled with love for you, Lord of Tanjore.
(2) Birāna nannélu kōrā Sri Brihadeshwara
Quickly protect me, Lord Brihadeshwara (=Śiva).

These four subsections were performed to the succession of *rāgas Tōḍi, Śaṅkarābharaṇam, Pantuvarāli* and *Aṭhānā*, with the intervening *Sollukaṭṭu* sections of *tirmānam*. Then, in place of a new verse for the *muktāyi* section, the four *rāgas* were performed in reverse order with *svara* vocalization, shifting the emphasis to improvisation of melodic designs.

The *caraṇa* was similarly organized as a *rāgamālikā*. Ponniah's original text comprised only two lines.[12] However, Alarmel Valli's performance tradition precedes those with a *svara* "text" in *rāga Bhairavī* as the refrain and this interpolated line:

Satíléni Kalyāṇī nenura
I am unrivalled as Kalyāṇī (in my beauty)

This is performed in *rāga Kalyāṇī,* an obvious cerebral play with music and text. The final, and original *caraṇa* text lines by Ponniah are:

Jālamu tseyaka léra
Don't play at being difficult.
Māti mātiki née kirtini né vinti.
Let me listen to praise songs of you, constantly.

These last lines are sung in *rāgas Vasanta* and *Mukhārī.* Then, to conclude the performance with a "garland of *svaras*," these four *rāgas* are sung without a poetic text, in reverse order and in a single extended phrase, an apotheosis of *rāgamālikā*.

The judicious selection of *rāgas* in a *rāgamālikā* enhances the reception of moods and meanings for the learned audience.[13] In addition to the *Kalyāṇī* imagery there are several other text/music relationships at this broad level of meaning. *Rāga Tōḍi* conveys the mood of appeal appropriate to its use for the *pallavi,* and *Śaṅkarābharaṇam* is an alternative designation for Śiva who is the subject of the text. For the convoluted purist's delight *rāga Pantuvarāli* belongs to the *meḷa* classification *Kāmavardhanī*, which means "to promote desire," matching in intent the first *anupallavi* line.

The *rāgamālikā* selections for this composition are entirely different musically from that of the earlier described *śabdam* by Vaḍivelu with Balasaraswati's choices. Instead of similarity in pitch-sets, the two groups of *rāgas* in this *pada varṇam* are characterized by extreme contrasts in their pitch-sets. Each group of four *rāgas* has one with a sharp fourth degree (Ma *tivra*). The *pallavi* opens with *rāga Tōḍi* which has four flattened (*kōmal*) pitches, and then shifts to *Śaṅkarābharaṇam* with all pitches "natural" (*suddha*). For the remainder of the first *rāgamālikā* and the entire sequence of *rāgas* in the *caraṇa*, each change of *rāga* requires three shifts in pitch alteration. This array of changes would seem to contradict the aesthetic requirement that the succession of *rāgas* be made with care so that there be neither too great a similarity nor contrast. Perhaps the groupings in this work may be justified on the grounds that the easy recognizability of these well-known *rāgas* and their suitability in matching text moods and imagery gives their order a desired effect.

Padam. The second half of the program opens with a series of *padams*, the only repeated dance form in the program. It is a genre entirely constructed on an *abhinaya* basis. There is no intrusion of the rhythmic tension brought about with dance mnemonics or abstraction of text and melody though solfege. The content is entirely fixed on a lovelorn heroine in various moods and illustrates the ambiguity of *śṛṅgāra rasa* (romance) with respect to secular and spiritual love. The passionate expressions extend to the erotic, but one is expected to "interpret this appeal in a more spiritual and philosophical vein, as the yearning of *jīvātma* for *Paramātma* (the individual soul for the All-soul), the desire for man to be united with God, the passionate entreaty of devotee to deity."[14]

Spiritual devotion, *bhakti*, is at the heart of Bharata Nāṭyam, as it is for all the Carnatic arts. Perhaps it is due to this underlying significance that *bhakti* is not usually listed as one of the *rasas*. Rather, "the advocates of Bhakti held it to be supreme by itself," that it encompasses all *rasas* and that they are *aṅgas*, subordinate branches of *bhakti*.[15] *Bhakti* is most often associated with the peaceful detachment of *śānta rasa*, an ideal spiritual attainment, yet the full range of devotional attitudes portrayed in dances such as the *pada varṇam* and *padam* illustrates the identity of *bhakti* with all other *rasas*: *śṛṅgāra* (love), *karuṇa* (pathos, compassion), *vīra* (heroism), *hāsya* (humor) and *adbhuta* (wonder). Even *raudra* (anger, fury) has its place, usually portrayed as a manifestation of this mood by the gods in their response to human and demonic actions. The earlier *padam* composer-poets, exemplified by Purandaradāsa (sixteenth century) and Muthutāṇḍavar, dealt with *bhakti* in its purer and more dignified spiritual sense. Then in the seventeenth century Kṣetrajña established the theme of romance and explicit sex as metaphors for devotion and created monuments of poetic artistry which have served as the basis for expressiveness in Bharata Nāṭyam ever since.

The *padam* text has a three-part structure of a *pallavi* couplet, *anupallavi* couplet and a *caraṇa* of one or more verses. The performance design generally matches this pattern, but may also vary considerably through line subdivision and the use of both contrasting and interrelated melodic phrases to create a musical structure bearing little resemblance to the text's organization. The *pallavi* and *anupallavi* may each have several different melodic ideas and the *caraṇa* will re-use some of these as well as introduce a new melody. Furthermore, a custom prevails for the higher melodic range *anupallavi* to be performed before the lower range *pallavi*, particularly for *padams* composed by Kṣetrajña.[16]

The general musical feature for the *padam* is that of relaxed lyricism carried out through a slow tempo which allows each text syllable to be explored for its maximum musical expression. The *padam* requires a unique singing mannerism in which syllables are performed "with a characteristic 'dragging' of the rhythm . . . governed by the ebb and flow of *svaras* and *gamakas* (ornaments) . . .without ever losing grip on the *tāla*."[17] The musicians are guided by the dancer, but have a heavy responsibility to create an expressive mood which inspires the dancer and appeals to the audience. Higgins wrote of the musicians' role in correlating text, melody and rhythm in a way which would "provide the dancer with a natural musical gesture which may be tranlated into physical motion through *abhinaya*."[18] This encourages a greater freedom in melodic improvisation for *padam* performances and emphasizes the musical symbols of "word-painting."

Jāvali Toward the end of the nineteenth century a light-hearted romantic dance composition, *jāvali,* was added to the program. It eases the attitudes of restraint and intensity of the preceding *padams*, moving at a faster tempo, having a less complex melodic organization and using *rāgas* which are more flexible in performance rules and may be Hindustani rather than Carnatic, such as *Behāg*. Like the *padam* it is dense in text presentation and requires only *abhinaya* of the dancer, focusing on the "earthy" topic of human desires in love.

Tillāna. Moving to the close of the program the content is further lightened with the *tillāna* which returns to the concept of abstract dance. A lively and simple melodic character predominates. Improvisation of a subtle and complex manner is not regarded as necessary for the melody, and the listener will find this resulting in redundancy. However, this is a setting for rhythmically complex drumming and choreography with a return to *sollukaṭṭu* chanting drawn from *mṛdaṅgam* mnemonics. *Sollukaṭṭu* recitation is always characterized by strongly articulated presentation which has the resulting effect of a vocalized percussion. The *naṭṭuvanar* has been silent through the *padams* and *jāvalis*, but now has the opportunity to provide a display of vocal tongue-twisters in a challenge to both dancer and drummer.

Śloka. The performance occasionally concludes with the peaceful mood of *bhakti* sung to a Sanskrit text, a *śloka* verse. It provides a final interpretive dance limited to gestures which are not rhythmically articulated. This is paralleled musically by the elimination of percussion and *tāla* organizaion. This *ālāpana* style provides the singer and melody instrumentalist with an introspective mannerism uncharacteristic of the other dance items. It is now becoming a practice to begin the performance with a *śloka*. One chosen by Alarmel Valli is Kālidāsa's *śloka* on Sarasvatī's Māṇikavīṇā (The Gem-studded Vīṇā) which was performed in a *rāgamālikā* setting.[19]

As expressed in the opening statement, it is essential to consider the music of Bharata Nāṭyam within the context of its dance. There is little purpose in isolating its music for comparison with concert performances. This only fixes upon it an attitude of the autonomy of music. The demands made upon music in dance have a fuller range in expressive, intellectual and spiritual presentation and creativity.

Rāga Pitch-Sets [20]

Śahāna

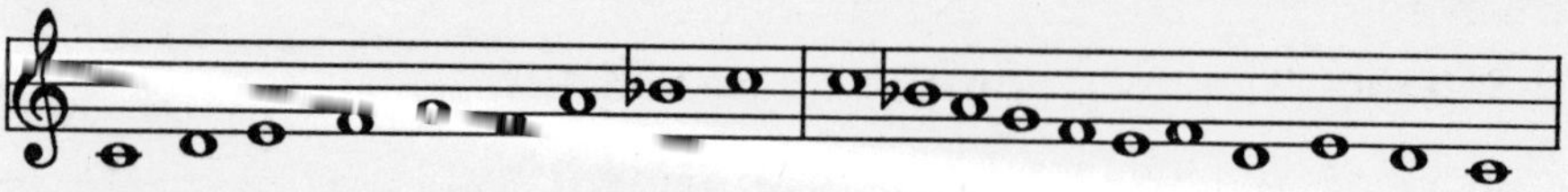

Punnāgavarāḷi

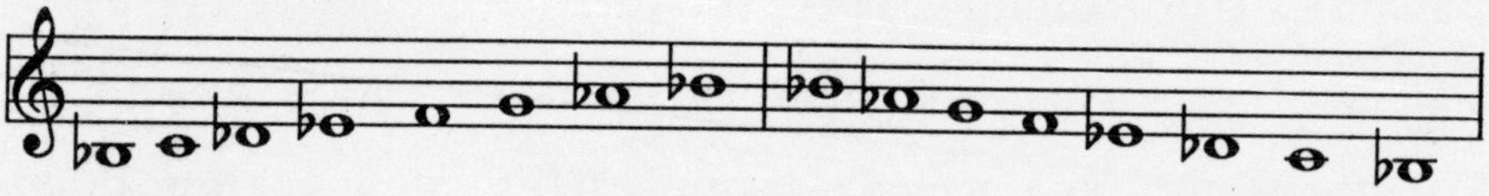

Khamās

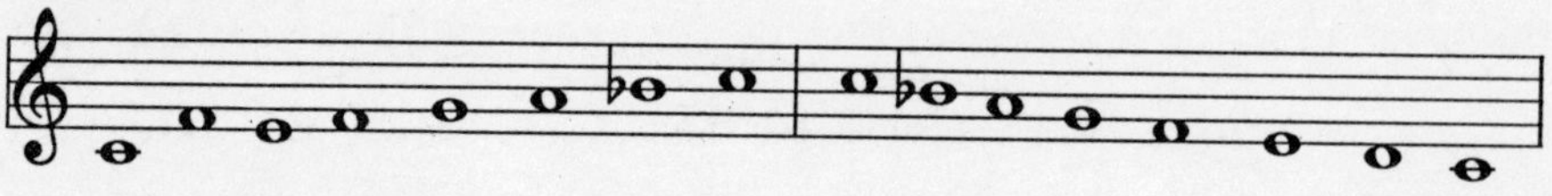

Nāṭakurañji

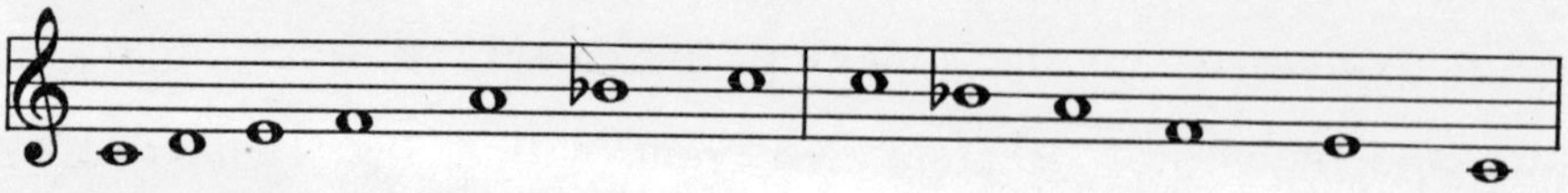

Kāmbhōji

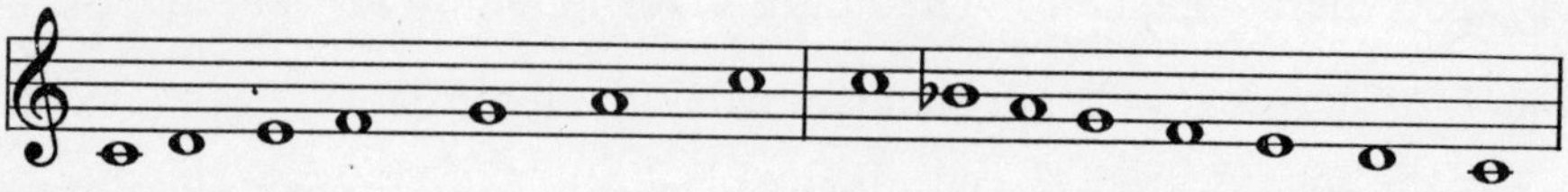

Suraṭi

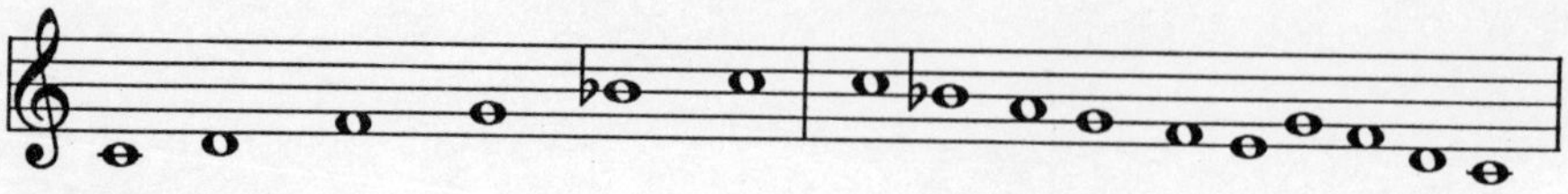

Bhairavī

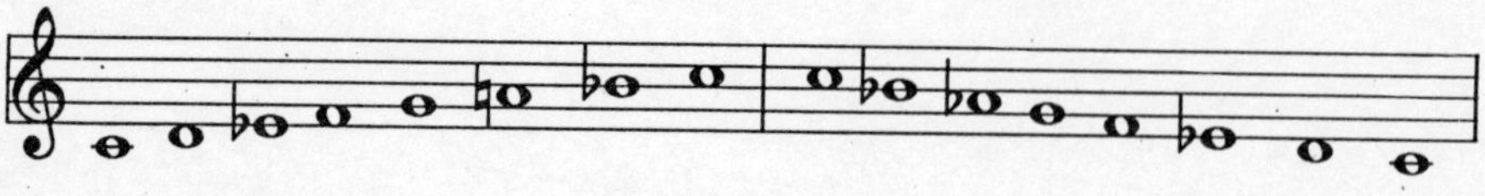

Tōḍi

Śaṅkarābharaṇam

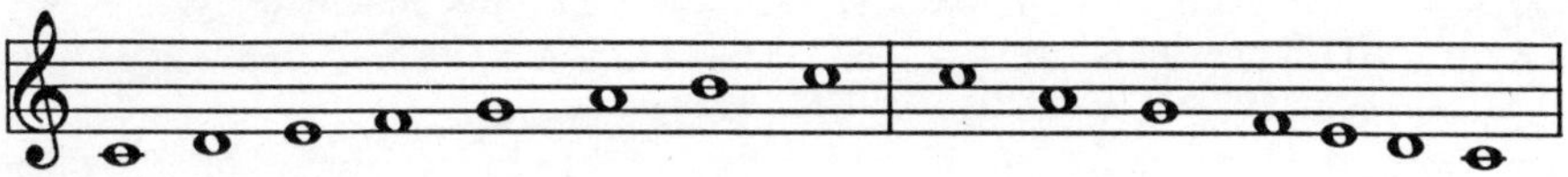

Pantuvarāli

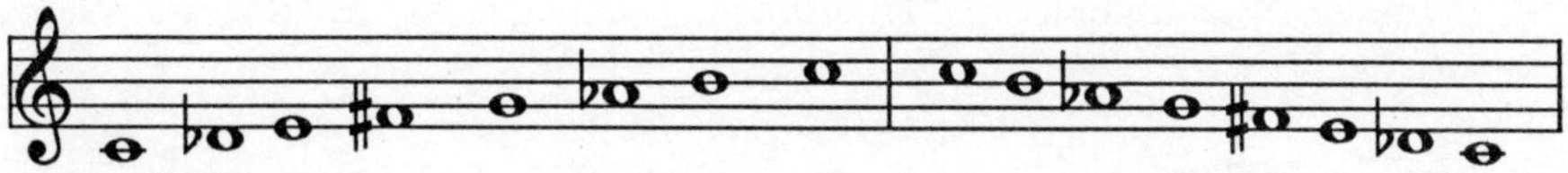

Aṭhānā

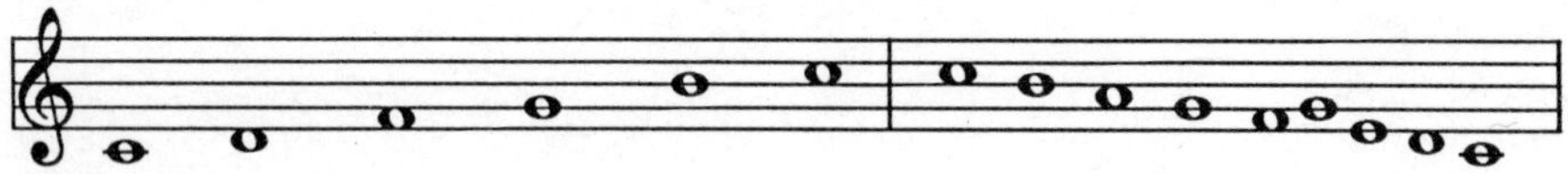

Kalyāṇī

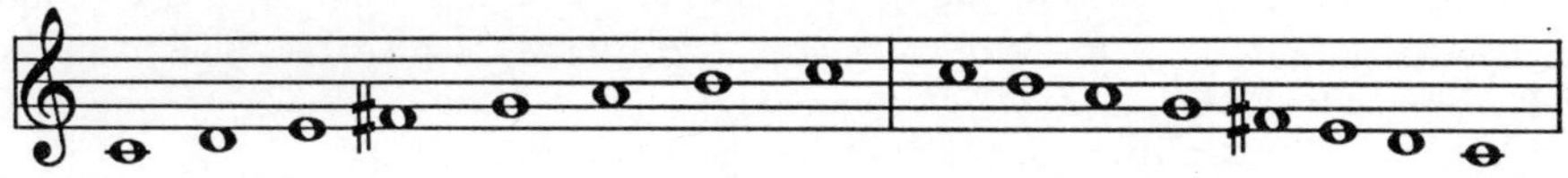

Vasanta

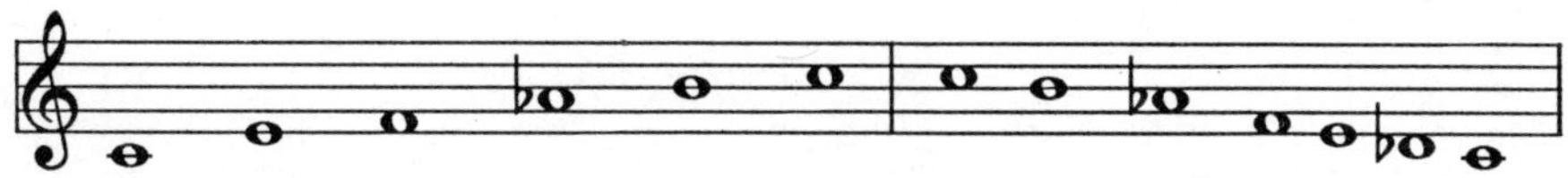

Mukhārī

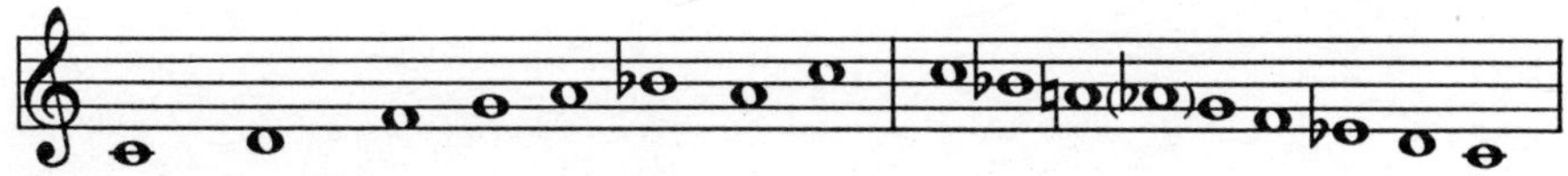

Notes

* American pioneer in the singing of Carnatic music and acknowledged as its first creditable Western performer. Jon Higgins' tragic and untimely death in 1984 has been a great loss to his friends, colleagues and students. The scholarly contribution of his unpublished doctoral dissertation, *The Music of Bharata Nāṭyam*, is of great significance to Indian music studies and it is both to this and his friendship that I wish to acknowledge my indebtedness.

1. Jon B. Higgins, *The Music of Bharata Nāṭyam*, (unpublished Ph.D. dissertation, Wesleyan University, 1973), p.11.
2. The most complete biography and collection of dance songs of the Tanjore Quartette is that of Tanjore K.P. Kittappa, *Thanjai Nalvar: Nattiya Isai Karuvoolam* [Tanjore Quartette: Compilation of Dance Music] (Madras, 1985).
3. Summary descriptions of the genres appear in Higgins, op. cit., pp. 27-28 and in Nirmala Ramachandran, "Traditional Compositions in Bharata Natyam," *Journal of the Music Accademy, Madras*, vol. 53 (1982), pp. 165-179.
4. Higgins, *The Music of Bharata Nāṭyam*, pp. 54 ff.
5. Performed on May 20, 1986 at the University of Minnesota, Minneapolis, under the sponsorship of Natyakala: Minnesota Society for South Asian Dance.
6. Higgins, *The Music of Bharata Nāṭyam*, pp. 107 ff.
7. Ibid., p. 105.
8. Ibid., p. 120.
9. Loc. cit.
10. See note 5.
11. Translation by Alarmel Valli.
12. Kittapa, *Thanjai Nalvar*, p. 138.
13. Cf. V.P. Dhananjayan, "Sringara and Bhakti in Dance," *Journal of the Music Academy, Madras*, vol. 54 (1983), pp. 206-208, in which there is a discussion of programming with respect to three audiences: *pāmara, paṇḍita* and *jñānī* (the layman, the educated and the enlightened).
14. Higgins, *The Music of Bharata Nāṭyam*, p. 139.
15. V. Raghavan, *The Number of Rasas*, 3rd rev. ed. (Madras: The Adyar Library and Research Centre, 1975), p. 142-143.
16. Higgins, *The Music of Bharata Nāṭyam*, p. 203.
17. Ibid., p. 211.
18. Ibid., p. 144.
19. May 18, 1986, Minneapolis, Minnesota.
20. These *rāga* pitch-sets are presented in the order they are referred to in this publication. The source used is Walter Kaufmann, *The Rāgas of South India*, (Bloomington, Indiana: Indiana University Press, 1976).

Bibliography

Dhananjayan, V.P., "Sringara and Bhakti in Dance," *Journal of the Music Academy, Madras,* vol. 54 (1983), pp. 206-208.

Higgins, Jon B., *The Music of Bharata Nāṭyam* (unpublished Ph.D. dissertation, Wesleyan University, 1973).

Kaufmann, Walter, *The Rāgas of South India* (Bloomington, Indiana: Indiana University Press, 1976).

Kittappa, Tanjore K.P., *Thanjai Nalwar: Nattiya Isai Karuvoolam* [Tanjore Quartette: Compilation of Dance Music] (Madras, 1985).

Raghavan, V., *The Number of Rasas*, 3rd rev. ed. (Madras: The Adyar Library and Research Centre, 1975).

Ramachandran, Nirmala, "Traditional Compositions in Bharata Natyam," *Journal of the Music Academy, Madras*, vol. 53 (1982), pp. 165-179.

V

Dynamics of Interaction Between Indian Dance and Sculpture

Michael Rabe

One of the hallmarks of Indian culture, one exemplified as much in the visual arts as by philosophical treatises, is the affirmation of an underlying unity behind the world of appearances. All phenomena, whether natural or man-made, are see as potential manifestations of an otherwise ineffable Ultimate Reality. The *advaitin,* or non-dualist, resorts to visual analogies to accomodate the diversities of life on earth with his monistic outlook: the single moon with its myriad reflections upon this watery planet; illusory circles of light when a fire brand is twirled. But characterization of the Many as reflections of the One need not imply denial of their individual worth. Even the greatest promulgator of Advaita monism, the eighth-century Śaṅkarācārya, is credited with also writing one of the most popular outpourings of *bhakti* to the goddess Pārvatī, the *Saundaryalaharī*, or *Flood of Beauty.*[1]

In the same spirit I propose to share a few reflections upon the nature of two still-more popularizing mediums of Hindu culture--dance and sculpture. Borrowing the metaphor of mirror-images from the famous treatise on Indian dance, the *Abhinaya Darpaṇa*, or *Mirror of Dramatic Expression*,[2] let us consider the extent to which essential aspects of each medium are mirrored in the other.

Obviously they share much in common as only a glance at twin depictions of the archetypal goddess or Naṭarāja (Plates 1 and 9, 3 and 10) will confirm. But how are the obviously common elements of attribute and pose to be accounted for? Are they perhaps nothing more than the accidental consequences of long coexistence within the same cultural milieu--twin pillars in the temple of Hindu ritual? Or are there factors inherent in each medium that have motivated the plastic and performing arts of India to emulate each other? Clearly there would be no reason for continuing this inquiry unless the latter question can be answered in the affirmative.

There are, in other words, good reasons why Indian classical dance should be characterized as having a propensity for the "sculpturesque".[3] It is no accident that in contrast to the more seamless flow of ballet, for example, the cadence of Bharata Nāṭyam tends to be punctuated by a series of discrete poses, for each of which the dancer's movement is momentarily arrested. Conversely, one need only recall the frequency with which images of dancing figures have been found from throughout the country to entertain the premise that Indian sculpture has been deeply infused by the verve and poetry of dance.

A second reason for introducing the metaphor of mirror-images is that it is reminiscent of another kind of looking-glass analogy. As a justification for religious art in the Eastern Orthodox church, icons have sometimes been likened to windows--through which the otherwise invisible presence of God may be seen.[4] at the risk of oversimplification, or inferring too much from the obvious difference between catching a reflection of oneself in a mirror and seeing something else through a window, it may be instructive to ponder the relative merits of both analogies as applied to the sister arts of dance and sculpture in the Indian context. for the empathetic viewer (the *sahṛdaya*, or "like-hearted" one), do they serve as mirrors or windows?

An appropriate point of departure for this exploration of the interconnectedness of dance and sculpture is provided by the framing narrative of a Gupta compendium on all the arts. The *Viṣṇudharmottara Purāṇa, Khaṇḍa* 3, opens with the request of a certain king Vajra to the *ṛṣi* Mārkaṇḍeya for instruction in the art of sculpture:

> Vajra: O sinless one, How should I make the forms of gods so that the image made according to rules may always manifest (the deity)?
>
> Mārkaṇḍeya: He who does not know the canon of painting (*citrasūtram*) can never know the canon of image-making (*pratimā lakṣaṇam*).
>
> Vajra: O scion of Bhṛgu Race, explain to me the canon of painting because one who knows the canon of painting, knows the canon of image-making.
>
> Mārkaṇḍeya: It is very difficult to know the canon of painting, without the canon of dance [*nṛtta śāstra*], because O king, in both, the world is to be imitated (or represented).
>
> Vajra: Explain to me the canon of dance and then you will speak about the canon of painting because O twice-born, one who knows the practice of the canon of dance knows painting.
>
> Mārkaṇḍeya: Dance is difficult to understand by one who is not acquainted with instrumental music (*ātodya*). Dance can in no way be known without it.

Vajra: O the knower of Law, speak about instrumental music and then you will speak about the canon of dance, because O excellent Bhārgava, when the instrumental music is properly understood, one understands dance.

Mārkaṇḍeya: O Acyuta, without vocal music [gīta], it is not possible to know instrumental music. One who knows the practice of the canon of vocal music, knows everything according to rules.

Vajra: Explain to me the canon of vocal music, O the best of the holders of the Law, because one who knows the canon of vocal music, is the best of men who knows everything.

Mārkaṇḍeya: Vocal music is two-fold--Sanskrita and Prākṛta and the third Apabhraṣṭa [vernaculars], however is infinite, O king, on account of the variety of local dialects, its limit cannot be determined in this world. Vocal music is to be understood as subject to recitation and recitation is done in two ways, Prose [*gadya*] and Verse [*padya*]. O knower of Law, Prose is as found in [everyday] conversation [*saṃkathā*] while verse is as in metre [*chanda*]. Metre is of many varieties.[5]

Thus in reverse order, the text's table of contents is introduced with the *unifying* rationale that mastery of each discipline is prerequisite to the study of the next. To the extent that the stylized dialogue reflects a cultural ideal, therefore, we can conclude that the sculptors of ancient India were expected to be thorougly versed in all the other arts, but particularly in dance. While this latter point is only implicit in the text, it follows from reflection upon the special kinship that exists between them. Only sculpture and dance, among the related arts enumerated by Mārkaṇḍeya, are devoted almost exclusively to communication through the human figure. They both speak the same "body language" so to say.

Speaking of language, it is vital to note that the *Viṣṇudharmottara* passage just quoted ultimately establishes poetics as the ground from which the other arts must be nourished. The significance of this predisposition of all Indian arts towards the poetic is that they tend as a consequence to be governed more strictly by stylizing conventions than are their counterparts in the West. Each discipline, including dance and sculpture, has its canonical ideals, the visual equivalents of meter, rhyme, alliteration and the other ornaments (*alaṃkāra*) of poetry. The centrality of these conventionalizing modes of expression is evident from the fact that the discipline of aesthetics in Sanskrit literature is called *alaṃkāra śāstra*, i.e., the study or craft of ornamentation.

Perhaps the first scholar to recognize the significance of this orientation was Ananda Coomaraswamy when he wrote of *nāṭya* (a term encompassing both dance and drama) as an essentially poetic art, an interpretation of life, while modern European theater is prose, or imitation of real experience.[6] This distinction may be applied with equal validity to the art of *śilpa,* or sculpture, as the following East-West comparison demonstrates.

Compared to the sinuous poetry of a Cōḷa-period Pārvatī (Plate 1), Auguste Rodin's first masterpiece, *The Age of Bronze* (1875-77, Plate 2) is halting prose.[7] Not that the latter is any less successfully realized, for indeed, both sculptures epitiomize the best of their respective traditions. But when the two are juxtaposed, one's jolting first impression is that the contours of Rodin's figure are disturbingly taut, its attitude distraught, compared to the preternatural fluidity of line and gracious demeanor of the South Indian goddess.

Further evaluation confirms the appropriateness of the prose versus poetry distinction as defined by both the *Viṣṇudharmottara* and Coomaraswamy. Rodin's *Age of Bronze* is "prosaic" in its factual approximation of a specific individual's appearance, notwithstanding the generalized reference of its title (to a "time of sorrow" after the passage of a Golden Age--a biblical Kali Yuga.[8]) So convincing is its anatomical realism, so devoid of idealizing convention, that some critics accused Rodin of casting it from life. Though the accusation was proven false (with photographs of the model who had posed for the sculpture) it was not so improbable as it may sound: European artists had been using plaster casts as *aide memoire* since at least the eighteenth century and the practice may even have originated in ancient Greece.[9]

The Pārvatī, on the other hand, is more a "poetic" evocation in that its form owes little to direct observation of actual human anatomy. Complex iconometric formulae, like the metrical rules of verse, have prescribed its elongated proportions and regulated the distribution of ornament. Pushing by the process of abstraction in the opposite direction from that taken by Rodin towards verisimilitude, the anonymous Indian master elicits admiration precisely for the unearthliness of the beauty he has conceived. Far from being concerned with factuality, he has instilled the figure with literary similies--a forehead shaped like the waxing moon, eyebrows that recall Kāma's bow, eyes like lotus buds or darting minnows, the impossibly long left arm, swinging free with the poise of an elephant's trunk.

Another major difference between them is that whereas *The Age of Bronze* is comparatively unique in subject matter, the Pārvatī is but one of a large class of virtually identical images. Here again, the *Viṣṇudharmottara's* insistence upon the interrelatedness of the arts is instructive. By analogy to the distinction, better known in music or dance, between the activities of composition and performance, one may say that while the Western sculptor concentrates his efforts in the former area, his Indian counterpart better exemplifies the latter. Consequently, the anonymous sculptor of the Pārvatī must be judged, like both the concert pianist and Bharata Nāṭyam dancer inevitably are, in terms of how well he has given expression to or "realized" a pre-existing composition. He cannot be faulted for lack of originality.

However, the distinction between composer and performer is not so mutually exclusive as it many sound. Even Rodin's comparatively novel conception recalls numerous earlier treatments of the striding nude warrior/athlete, among which the spear-bearing *Doryphoros* of Polykleitos (ca. 440 B.C.) is certainly the definitive "canon" or standard. Rodin's consciousness of that heritage against which his contribution to the genre would be judged is evident from the fact that he had first placed a spear in the figure's left hand, calling it "The Vanquished" (in reference to France in 1871). He later removed the spear and changed the sculpture's title in order to universalize its message--not to disguise its sources in the Classical Western tradition.

Conversely, the Indian sculptor exercised considerable latitude in his selection and rendering of time-honored canons of proportion and iconography. His opportunities for inventiveness were not unlike those of the concert pianist, who might introduce a cadenza of his own creation between movements of the inherited score; or those of the Bharata Nāṭyam dancer, who combines the traditional *aḍavus* into new compositions. While the greatest scope for innovation was in the design and distribution of jewelry, even more meaningful attributes might be introduced or eliminated at the artist's discretion. Two examples may be cited here, both of which have literary parallels in the *Saundaryalaharī*. First, as if to accentuate the figure's precariously thin waist, it has been marked by three horizontal creases which recall this passage from Śaṅkara's catalog of Pārvatī's charms:

> Slender by nature, wearied from the burden of your overhanging breasts,
> with bent form that seems to be cracking slightly at the navel and the abdominal creases--
> ever to your waist, which no more than a tree on the trembling rim of a torrent
> has any stability, may there ever be safety, O daughter of the mountain.
> ...
> Kāma trying to save your waist from breaking, O Devī,
> bound it, three-folded as it is, triply as with the withes of the lavalī creeper.[10]

The Pārvatī image in Plate 1 is of course not the only one to show the three abdominal creases, but they are sufficiently rare to exemplify the exercise of creative discretion.[11]

The second example of creative choice being exercised by the maker of the Tanjore Gallery Pārvatī is evident in the alignment of the figure's torso. Like all other spouse-goddesses of the type,[12] she stands in *tribhaṅga,* triple-bend contrapposto. As always, one arm is shown hanging free (in *dola hasta*, or in a swing-like pose) and the other is raised at the elbow in *siṃhakarṇa* (lion's ears)[13] to hold a lotus blossom. (The latter, incidentally, is an instance of the double-entendre richness that permeates so much Indian art. The lion's ears-like extension of the outer fingers recalls the ferocious side of the goddess in her independent form as Durgā--the *lion*-riding, multi-armed slayer of the Buffalo demon.) The Tanjore figure of Plate 1 also exemplifies the norm by having the lotus-holding *siṃha-karṇa mudrā* in her right hand, but differs from the majority in that her torso is inclined in the opposite direction, to proper left. The significance of this departure from the norm presupposes recognition of these prevailing conventions:

(1) This standing, two-armed form is standard for all goddesses in South India when they are shown as spouses; in other words, in all cases, except when they appear as the four-armed sovereigns of their own Śakti cult.

(2) Typically they stand to their husband's left side, and as if to register acceptance of that subordinate position, they hold the lotus on his side, i.e., in their right hands. When a second wife is in attendance (e.g., Bhūdevī with Viṣṇu and Lakṣmī), and must be

placed to his right, the lotus changes hands so as to preserve the semblance of sharing its fragrance with him.

(3) Similarly, as a further expression of conjugal rapport, the spouse-goddess inclines her torso towards her husband--usually towards the right (except, again, for second wives on the opposite side who must lean in to the left).[14]

Returning to the Tanjore Pārvatī of Plate 1, we see that it cannot fulfill both conditions two and three: the lotus-holding *mudrā* and torso-inclination are in opposite directions. If the sculpture portrays a dutiful wife sharing her lotus charms (both literal and figurative) with a husband on her right, why does she lean away from his implied presence? Or, in the less likely event that it is intended to depict a second wife leaning towards her husband from his right side, why hold the lotus away from him? The apparent anomaly disappears if the figure is identified as Pārvatī in a more specific context--as consort of Śiva in his Naṭarāja manifestation. When the goddess accompanies The Lord of Dance she is called Śivakāmasundarī (Śiva's Beloved Beauty). Positioned to his left, she is typically posed like the figure in Plate 1--with *siṃhakarṇa* in the right hand (on his side) and leaning away to the left.[15] In the absence of any other explanation in the literature for this atypical configuration of details, I offer the following three.

First, in purely formal terms, the outward inclination of her torso places it in sympathetic alignment with the broadly flaring *tiruvāci*, or firey nimbus (Plate 3) when she stands to the Naṭarāja's left..[16]

Second, it may not be wrong also to read a trace of jealousy in this withdrawing stance, for as the name Śivakāmi emphasizes, she is Śiva's passionate love--and hence the sight of the goddess Gaṅgā playfully tumbling through his hair (Plate 3) is cause for momentary alarm. Though the ascription of jealousy to Pārvatī at the sight of the descending Ganges is both ancient and still widely "celebrated"--as part of the standard repertoire in Bharata Nāṭyam expositions of the *Saundaryalaharī*, for example[17]--including of the "offending" presence of Gaṅgā in the locks of Śiva's hair is said to have a specific historical precedent. The motif was first introduced on Cōḷa bronzes during the reign of Rajendra I, in the second quarter of the eleventh century, after his victorious army returned from North India with vessels of Ganges water borne upon the heads of defeated kings.[18] Its exclusive association with only Naṭarāja images thereafter (at least among the bronzes of South India) can be explained as a lingering consequence of this imperial connotation--for Śiva Naṭarāja was the Cōḷa dynasty's *kula deva,* or patron deity *par excellence.*

The third contributing factor that may serve to explain Pārvatī's pose when she accompanies Naṭarāja as Śivakāmasundarī is also psychological and rooted in myth.[19] According to the *Sthala Purāṇa* of Tiruvālaṅkāṭu (a site thirty kilometers north of Kāñcīpuram), Kālī, the wrathful manifestation of Pārvatī, after feasting insatiably upon the blood of demons, threatened to devour all living creatures. In a bid to subdue Śiva as well, she challenged him to a dance contest. Śiva agreed and began dancing in modes prescribed by the *Sāmaveda*. Imitating him step by step, and perceiving his growing fatigue, the goddess grew overconfident and readily agreed to intensify the pace. But then Śiva assumed cosmic proportions and with one constellation-scattering kick to the heavens, proceeded with the dance known to iconographers as the *ūrdhva tāṇḍava*[20] Alternate versions of the myth differ as to whether Kālī was thrown powerless to the ground by the force of Śiva's cosmic dance, or was simply unwilling to imitate a pose she considered unbecoming, but in either case she conceded defeat. Consequently, in reward for resumption of a submissive guise, she was promised a position of honor to the side of the Naṭarāja, whenever he should dance in the future. Though this myth is localized at Tiruvālaṅkāṭu, it is sufficiently well-known[21] for us to presume that a hint of that erstwhile rivalry survives in every image of Śivakāmasundarī that leans away from rather than toward the Naṭarāja it accompanies.

If one should question the validity of such a multifaceted reading of an icon (or a dancer posed as one), it may be justified by returning to the central point of Mārkaṇḍeya's dialogue with king Vajra. Poetry is the ground from which all other arts are nourished. As compensation for accepting the formal constraints of convention, India's visual and performing arts have gained increased capacity for poetic suggestion--for *dhvani,* or resonance, as the *alaṃkāra śāstras* term it. Standard *mudrās*, for example, inevitably recall many previous encounters the viewer has had with them. They were codified precisely because of their potentiality for multiple meanings. Thus the so-called *siṃhakarṇa mudrā*, alternatively identified in dance treatises as *kaṭakāmukha* (opening in a link), may be used to suggest the picking of flowers, holding a string of pearls or garland, drawing a bow, distributing betel leaves, applying unguents, speech and glancing[22]--all these in addition to the previously cited holding of a lotus and premonition of Durgā's lion. While only one of them may be the intended meaning in a given context, the auxiliary associations can heighten the visual impact, like the timbre-enriching overtones produced by a *vīṇā's* sympathetic strings. Such nuances are not, of course, exclusive to the more "poetic" arts of the East, but they are probably less consequential in those stylistic traditions that favor a more prose-like naturalism. To the degree that Indian dance and sculpture are both highly stylized art forms, it is appropriate to characterize them as equally poetic in this sense.

A second aspect of Indian culture generally that may be seen as having a bearing on the interrelationships between dance and sculpture is theological. Popular Hinduism, is much of its literary, ceremonial and visual expressions is unabashedly life-affirming--a celebration of "the gods with us" in the here and now. Great emphasis is invariably placed, the "*neti-neti*" disclaimers of Advaita notwithstanding,[23] upon the dynamic life-cycle of *becoming* rather than on transcendental, non-qualified *being*. Lip service may always be paid to *mokṣa*[24] as an ultimate *summum bonum*, but attention tends to be concentrated upon immanent manifestations of the divine. This ambivalence towards the impersonal Ultimate Reality, concomitant with heart-felt yearning for God as a lover of very human souls, is especially distinctive of South India--the region that, not coincidently, has preserved such strong traditions of temple dance and theater. To cite only two examples:

Kāraikkāl Ammaiyār (ca. sixth century), the earliest historical devotee of Śiva-Naṭarāja, dutifully requested *mokṣa* in one of her hymns, but the more ardent plea was to be granted perpetual audience by The Lord of Dance:

> Grant unto me freedom from birth. But if it is Thy wish that I should be born again, grant me the boon that I should always be conscious of Thee. One more boon I ask of Thee, O lord of Dharma: it is that when Thou performest Thy cosmic dance, I may witness it standing near Thy feet.[25]

In Kaṃban's Tamil recasting of the *Rāmāyaṇa* (ca. twelfth century), the beauty of the natural world is extolled as capable of making one forget the supernatural. At dawn, for example:

> The sun whose death the day before recalled the death of all who suffer endless rebirths, the sun which is without birth was born again and thus made one forget heaven and all other pure worlds.[26]

Given this premise, that mainstream Hinduism focuses essentially upon *immanent* manifestations of the divine, it follows that symbolic expressions of dynamic *activity* should be more prevalent than images of transcendent stasis. In contrast to the Byzantine "icon-window" depictions of an unchanging Creator who came into the world but is not part of it, in both Śaiva and Vaiṣṇava Hinduism, the supreme deity is known from innumerable local manifestations--ultimately all life is an expression of His own *līlā*, or sporting recreation.

If, therefore, images of time- and space-bound activity are sought by the iconographer, what could be more natural than to incorporate into statuary the language of dance? Taking the argument a step further, the enshrining of dance itself as a vital medium of sacred ritual is perfectly consistent with a theology that stresses immanence. Both the visual and performing arts are charged with the task of facilitating *darśana*--visions of *līlā*, the divine comedy. Since the predominant myths of Hinduism emphasize the *activities* of God, it is inevitable that means to capture a sense of the dynamic will be sought.

This is one of the chief reasons, in my opinion, for the multiplicity of limbs that are ascribed to Indian deities.[27] A supreme case in point is the great eighteen-armed Naṭarāja on the facade of Bādāmi Cave I (mid-sixth century, Plate 4). Since images of supreme deity are most often visualized with four arms, the additional fourteen convey a spellbinding sense of continuous motion. Simultaneously, their distinctive attributes and *mudrās* impart a range of meaning that is analogous to an extended sequence of a dancer's gestures in real time. However far afield a comparison to early twentieth-century painting may appear, it was exactly this challenge--the attempt to capture a sense of the kinetic (time as the fourth dimension[28])--that motivated early Futurist and Cubist experiements like Marcel Duchamp's *Nude Descending a Staircase*.

A sense of the kinetic is also implicit in orthodox interpretations of the more standard, four-armed Naṭeśa images (Plate 3). Each arm portrays a different one of the divine *kriyās* (activities): viz., creation, by the emanation of sound from the drum;

destruction, by the flames in the opposite hand; preservation in between these polarities, expressed by the *abhaya mudrā* of reassurance; obscuring of truth (temporarily, at least), by the *gaja hasta* (elephant's trunk-like gesture) of the arm thrown across the chest. Finally, the up-raised foot to which the *gaja hasta* casts a veiled reference, is said to represent the fifth *kriyā*--liberation from ignorance (personified by the dwarf Muyalaka underfoot).[29]

Corollary evidence that multiple arms in Hindu sculpture were at least partially inspired by the dynamism inherent in dance appears in the scholarly discussion of the Bṛhadīśvara *karaṇa* reliefs. The Bhṛhadīśvara is the major temple of Tanjore, built in the early eleventh century, during the reign of the great Cōḷa emperor, Rājarāja I. Lining the inner walls of a circumambulatory corridor, one floor above the inner sanctum, there is an extensive series of basrelief panels which depict a four-armed Śiva dancing to the accompaniment of drumming provided by his *gaṇa* attendants. According to the fourth chapter of the *Nāṭyaśāstra*, Śiva revealed to its author, Bharata, 108 *karaṇas*, or elemental movements of the arms and legs, from which all possible dance sequences may be composed.[30] Though the Bṛhadīśvara series was never completed, the 81 panels which are extant have been found to coincide in serial order to the first three-quarters of these textually defined *karaṇas*. Since Śiva in each panel is depicted with two pairs of arms, some interpreters have attempted to correlate them with multiple phases in a sequence of movements.[31] Whether or not this literal correspondence between text, practice and sculpture was actually intended, there is no doubt but that the overall visual effect of multiple limbs is one of heightened dynamism.

Two other attributes of the quintessential Naṭarāja bronzes further enhance the sense of dynamism that multiple limbs establish--the gyrating *jaṭās* (dread locks) and the *tiruvāci* (nimbus). The former, matted coils of hair braided with flowers, are reminiscent of the blur of spokes around a wheel's theoretically motionless center. By their centrifugal extension about the face they intensify by contrast its aura of beatific calm. As for the *tiruvāci*, or flame-fringed halo, much as been written on its symbolism in both traditional Tamil sources and by art historians.[32] Superficially, it does not differ from the *prabhāvalī*, the "arc of glory" that surrounds any number of other images from throughout the country. But on a more esoteric level, for Naṭarāja in particular, it is said to signify the dance of Prakṛti, or Nature, in contrast to the dance of primordial Puruṣa, or Spirit within. As such it recalls the famous *Sāṅkhya-kārikā*:

> As the dancer desists from dancing, having exhibited herself to the audience, so does [Prakṛti] Primal Matter desist, having exhibited herself to [Puruṣa] the Spirit.[33]

The key difference in this Śaiva context is that the witnessing Spirit is not a passive audience of Nature but Primordial Cause that is also dancing at the center of the encircling matter. Thus one can imagine the firey nimbus as generated from that single flame in Śiva's upper left hand. In other words, there is only a single flame present but the illusion of many is created sequentially as in a time-lapse photograph. Paradoxically, the one flame, symbolic of destruction, gives rise to the *māyā* (illusion) of many, symbolic of creation. The metaphor of an illusory circle produced by rotating a firebrand can be traced back to early Buddhist texts which used it to explain away the sense of continuity in human personality.[34] Early Advaitic texts, like the *Gauḍapāda Kārikā* further popularized the metaphor while reversing its emphasis to stress solitary existence of pure consciousness.[35] But regardless of whether the Ultimate should be defined in negative or positive terms (as Nirvāṇa or Brahman), in the phenomenal realm, an illusory circle produced by keeping a single flame in motion remains an effective symbol of the kinetic, its appearance in sculpture reflecting awareness and emulation of the temporal dimension of dance.

Turning the dance-sculpture equation around, let us now try to explain what has been called the "sculpturesque quality" of Indian classical dance. Why has such prominence been given in Bharata Nāṭyam to the sequential display of momentarily stationary poses? Why is the dancer, in the words of Kapila Vatsyayan, "constantly trying to achieve the perfect pose which will convey a sense of timelessness."[36]

The most straightforward answer, the affirmation that dance has consciously been shaped in terms of a sculptural aesthetic, was first recorded in the sixteenth century by a Portuguese visitor to the Vijayanagar court. Domingo Paes described a performance hall as decorated with carvings of various dance poses for the express purpose of instructing the dancing girls:

> The designs of these panels show the positions at the ends of dances in such a way that on each panel there is a dancer in the proper position at the end of the dance; this is to teach the women, so that if they forget the position in which they have to remain when the dance is done, they may look at one of the panels where is the end of that dance. By that way they keep in mind what they have to do.[37]

However simplistic this practical explanation of typical *nāṭyaśālā* (performance hall) iconography may sound, it is not easily dismissed as naive conjecture. His reference to poses held at the end of dance sequences not only anticipates Vatsyayan's reference to the "timeless pose," but implies acquaintance with the *Nāṭyaśāstra* codification of *karaṇas* already alluded to.

Due to the extreme brevity of the *karaṇa* definitions provided by Bharata, uncertainties with respect to their execution and relevance to actual performance have persisted in subsequent literature. Many of the official 108 are rarely utilized by dancers today and others are interpreted in more than one way. Because of these uncertainties in text and practice, several complete sets of sculptural renderings of the *karaṇas* have gained an importance that perhaps exceeds their original purpose. Except for the incomplete series that rings the sanctuary at Tanjore, the others are arranged in tall vertical tiers along the inner passageways of *gopurams*, or temple gateways, at Cidambaram (Plates 7, 8), Kumbakoṇam, Tiruvaṇṇāmalai and Vṛddhāchalam. Because of the inaccessibility of the upper ones for convenient study, they must have been primarily decorative or symbolic rather than didactic in intent--auspicious charms guarding the gates, welcoming the faithful. Still, the very existence of these sculptural renderings suggests the possibility that dancers, since at least the Cōḷa period, have had access to comparable illustrations, perhaps in manuscript form. It may also be inferred that over the centuries these visual records exerted a conservative influence, retarding innovation, since visual depictions are much less susceptible than written texts to the vagaries of an expositor's imagination. The *karaṇa* reliefs on all four *gopurams* at Cidambaram must have been especially influential due to their association with Śiva-Naṭarāja. It is there in mythic time and eternally that Śiva performs the *ānanda tāṇḍava* dance. Their authoritative status is further underscored by the fact that on the principal East and West gates each panel is inscribed with its corresponding definition from the *Nāṭyaśāstra*.

But a more fundamental aspect of the question remains: did these sculptural depictions serve merely as passive or conceptually neutral conduits of *nāṭya* technique from one generation to the next, or did the sculpture medium itself exercise a transmogrifying effect on dance even while preserving it? In other words, were dancers increasingly prone to rigidify their movements, to hold static positions in emulation of stone images, rather like alchemists slowly embalming themselves by drinking mercury-laced elixirs? In short, did the preserving medium of sculpture "infect" the style, if not also the content of the performance medium being preserved? In my opinion, the answer is yes on both counts.

The likelihood of this "petrification" process having occurred seems probable from the following consideration. As the performer of any classical dance or musical tradition knows, it is essential to maintain rapport with one's audience. To do so one must draw upon the connoisseur's knowledge of the discipline. Given the highly esoteric sign language of Bharata Nāṭyam it is only natural that special use should be made of the most familiar poses. And what could the temple dancer count upon her audience having greater familiarity with than the *karaṇas* framed so prominently on the gates and dance chamber pillars? To insure recognition of her accomplishments she would necessarily be inclined to emphasize those stages of a cadence of movements that sculptors had previously sanctioned as most characteristic.

On a still more basic level, the influence of sculpture on dance can be demonstrated by showing that some of the *karaṇas* originated in iconography. They were apparently adapted into the repertoire of dance as abbreviated references to specific myths for which poses had already been standardized for sculpture.

A prime example is the pose associated almost exclusively with Śiva's *ānanda tāṇḍava*, the cosmic dance associated with Cidambaram and most frequently depicted in statuary (Plate 3). In the *Nāṭyaśāstra* at least three *karaṇas* incorporate its distinctive kick of one leg up across the other. The first and basic version called *Bhujaṅgatrāsita* (Frightened by a Serpent) is *karaṇa* 24. Its variants are *karaṇas* 35 and 40, called *Bhujaṅgatrasta Recita* (Reeling with Serpent Fright) and *Bhujaṅgāñcita* (Serpent Touch) respectively. The derivation of all three poses (which differ only in the disposition of the hands) from sculpture rather than the other way around seems implicit from their names. In contrast to the more generic terminology by which key movements of many other *karaṇas* are identified,[38] these three manifestations of "serpent fright" recall the foundation myth of the Cidambaram temple. According to the *Cidambaram āhātmya*, a coterie of atheistic ascetics dwelling in the Tillai forest failed to recognize Śiva and tried to frighten him away with creatures conjured from their sacrificial fire.[39] One of these was the serpent which caused Śiva to recoil in mock alarm, before picking it up for a bracelet and beginning to dance. Significantly, the oldest extant Naṭarāja in Tamil Nadu, in the sixth-century cave temple at Śiyamaṅgalam (Plate 5) is already associated with that ineffectual serpent, prominently underfoot, giving rise to the *Bhujaṅgatrāsita* pose.

The priority of sculptural formulations over actual performance of the *bhujaṅga karaṇas* is further evident from the disparity which exists between the frenetic activity implicit in the term *tāṇḍava* by which Śiva's dancers are classified,[40] and their rather sedate definitions in the *Nāṭyaśāstra*. The definition of *Bhujaṅgatrāsita*, for example, is a better description of the standard *ānanda tāṇḍava* icon than it is a prescription for an actual sequence of leaping movements:

> Lift up the bent leg, turn the thigh in Tryaśra, and keep the waist and knees arched out.[41]

The fact that contemporary dancers also evoke the presence of Naṭarāja by momentarily assuming the definitive iconic pose (Plate 10), rather than by vigorous movement in a *tāṇḍava* mode, only underscores the normative influence of sculpture upon their medium.

Another icon-inspired *karaṇa* is no. 100, called *Viṣṇukrānta*. Bharata's description of "Viṣṇu's Stride" is characteristically terse:

> The legs are stretched in front and bent as though in preparation for walking. The two hands are in Rēcita.[42]

But as with *Bhujaṅgatrāsita*, the *karaṇa's* name itself is suggestive enough: *Viṣṇukrānta* clearly refers to Viṣṇu's Vāmana incarnation which culminated in the triple-step across the universe (Plate 6) for which iconography has been formalized by sculptors by at least the fifth century. It was the emulation of Trivikrama-Viṣṇu (Viṣṇu encompassing the universe--earth, space, sky--in three steps) sculptures that dictated for dance the stiff extension of the raised leg and corresponding arm (Plate 8). And it is in order to sustain this awkward, statue-like position that dancers sometimes grab hold of the extended foot.[43]

Several other poses in the repertoire of contemporary classical dance may be shown to derive from sculptural antecedents without the mediation of specific textual warrant. The pure *nṛtta* pose on the frontispiece of this book, for example, recalls innumerable *śālabhañjikās,* or tree-*yakṣīs* that have adorned the sacred monuments of India, irrespective of creed, for the last two millenia.[44] The hand-clasp over head and the continuous arc defined by the left arm and torso are reminiscent of a *yakṣī's* posture when hanging from a lower branch of the tree to which she is giving a fructifying kick.

Similarly, the popularity of the *mṛdaṅgam* drumming pose in Odissi is said to be inspired by the numerous carved figures of musicians that appear on the dance hall and atop the *vimāna* (sanctuary) of the temple at Konārak.[45] So too the more frequent assumption of the *tribhaṅga* (triple-axis) contrapposto may be attributed to a more conscious evocation of iconographic sanction.[46] Yet even in Bharata Nāṭyam it is common enough (Plate 9), particularly in the representation of consort goddesses, to cite it as another example of arrested movement, sculpturesque in both origin and intent.

Nevertheless, care must be taken to avoid overdrawn conclusions. One could legitimately argue that all the examples of sculpture-derived poses in dance are exceptions to a more general rule that most of the movements and gestures of Bharata Nāṭyam have no true equivalents in the visual arts--except when the exchange is in the other direction--when deities are shown dancing. The essential independence of most *abhinaya* or dance-pantomime from sculptural sources can be illustrated by *karaṇas* 1 and 68 in the *Nāṭyaśāstra*. *Talapuṣpapuṭa* (Palms Cupped with Flowers, Plate11) is first on the list because it corresponds to the invocation at the start of a *nāṭya* performance.[47] Invariably the dancer, or *sūtradhāra* (master of ceremonies) in the case of multicharacter dramas, scatters flowers in homage to the stage, its attending deities and the audience. Being such an integral item of Bharata Nāṭyam, it must certainly have developed independently of any sculptural antecedent. In the rare cases where it does occur as a *mudrā* in sculpture,[48] it is scarcely distinguishable from *añjali*, the *mudrā* of salutation. But the two are distinguishable, and again, it is the *karaṇa*'s name, specifying in this case the offering of flowers, which is indicative of its origin--in the theater.

The other *karaṇa* which illustrates the essential independence of dance movements from sculptural iconography is no. 68, called *Gajakrīḍita* (Playing Like An Elephant). According to Bharata's text:

> The left hand is arched over the ear, the right is placed in Latā Hasta and the legs in Dōla Pāda. [49]

In other words, an elephant's swaying gait is enhanced by fanning the left arm like one of its ears and the other like a trunk. In Bharata Nāṭyam this *karaṇa* is still used to identify the elephant-headed Gaṇeśa (Plate 12). As such it is an example of mime inspired by the look and movement of real elephants, not Gaṇeśa statues. If the latter were the operative source one might expect instead to see the definition of corpulence with a broad sweep of both hands or the holding of his chief attributes, the severed tusk (which he uses as a writing stylus) and a bowl of sweets.

In view of the evidence on both sides, therefore, a judicious middle position is best taken with respect to the degree of influence sculpture has exerted upon dance in India. Simply stated, and incidentally this is the opinion expressed by several Bharata Nāṭyam dancers themselves, the truth of the matter seems to be that no matter how minimal the emulation of sculpture may have been historically, it has significantly increased in recent years. Anne-Marie Gaston, for example, has written of the inspiration she received to study Bharata Nāṭyam after visiting Cidambaram, and Odissi, likewise, after seeing the Sun Temple at Konārak[50]. She has also noted that others are choreographing new dances with poses derived from sculptural sources. Doubtless the best example of this trend has been the crusade of Padma Subrahmanyam to reintroduce all 108 *karaṇas* of the *Nāṭyaśāstra* into the contemporary repertoire after writing a doctoral dissertation on the subject.[51] At least one dancer has followed suit: Swarnamukhi has won acclaim precisely for her ability to perform all 108 *karaṇas*.

Explanations for this phenomenon have to do with cultural changes in the twentieth century. Firstly, the absolute authority of the traditional *guru* has diminshed--no longer are one or two chosen disciples able to spend many years in the master's household. Young dancers, like the students of other disciplines, ineveitably become more eclectic in their training, more receptive to innovation. Secondly, an increased awareness of the diversity of sculptural representations of dance has been a natural consequence of increased means and frequency of travel and image reproduction by photography. Even if dancers were fully conversant with their idiom's potential without recourse to the visual arts, there remains the ever-increasing familiarity of their audience with published illustrations which serve as a natural pool of collective imagery to draw upon when seeking to elicit *rasāsvāda*, or soulful appreciation of their art.

To conclude this exploration of some interactions between dance and sculpture, let us return to looking-glass metaphor. We have seen that both arts offer illuminating reflections of the other--that sculptors have often sought to evoke in their icons a dance-inspired kinetic quality, while dancers have returned the compliment, as it were, by striking sculpturesque poses. At the outset we questioned the relative merits of two different looking-glass analogies--the window and the mirror. In my opinion the former is more suited to sculpture and the latter to dance. The Orthodox justification of sacred icons as windows through which one encounters God is just as applicable to Hindu aspirations in temple worship. In both traditions, the aspirant looks to them in hope of *darśana*, a vision of God who is Other. Dancers, on the other hand, are more mirror-like. In the mystical encounter between God and man, Bharata Nāṭyam dancers, though sometimes playing divine roles, invariably remain on the human side--even when as *devadāsīs* they were ceremonially married to temple images. Therefore, when the viewer of her performance partakes vicariously in the *rasa* of her emotions, it is like seeing one's own soul reflected in the *abhinaya darpaṇa*, the mirror of dramatic expression.

Colorplate I. Alarmel Valli in *nṛtta* pose; raised hand in *sikhara hasta*, extended hand in *patāka hasta*.
Photo: Thomas Foley.

Colorplate II. Alarmel Valli in *nṛtta* pose; both hands in *alapadma hasta*. Photo: Thomas Foley.

Colorplate III. Alarmel Valli in *nṛtta* pose; right hand in *dola hasta*, left hand in *arāla hasta*. Photo: Thomas Foley.

Colorplate IV. Alarmel Valli in *nṛtta* pose; both hands in *haṃsāsya hasta*. Photo: Thomas Foley.

Colorplate V. Alarmel Valli in *abhinaya* pose; both hands in *padmakośa hasta*, joined at the wrists, symbolizing the opening of a lotus. Photo: Thomas Foley.

Colorplate VI. Alarmel Valli in *abhinaya* pose; right hand in *alapadma hasta*, left hand in *bhramara hasta*, jointly representing the kiss. Photo: Thomas Foley.

Colorplate VII. Alarmel Valli in *abhinaya* pose; both hands in *patāka hasta*, one superimposed on the other, symbolizing waiting. Photo: Thomas Foley.

Colorplate VIII. Alarmel Valli in *abhinaya* pose, representing love in separation. Photo: Thomas Foley.

Notes

1. *The Saundaryalaharī, or Flood of Beauty: Traditionally Ascribed to Śaṅkarācārya*, edited and translated by W. Norman Brown (Cambridge, Massachusetts: Harvard University Press, 1958).

2. *The Mirror of Gesture: Being the Abhinaya Darpaṇa of Nandikeśvara*, translated into English by Ananda Coomaraswamy and Gopala Kristnayya Duggirala, 1917 reprint ed. (New Delhi: Munshiram Manoharlal, 1970).

3. E.g., Ram Gopal, *Indian Dancing* (Bombay: Asian Publishing House, 1951), p. 36.

4. For discussion of this issue I am grateful to Robert Kleinhans, Professor of Religious Studies, Saint Xavier College, Chicago.

5. *Viṣṇudharmottara Purāṇa, Third Khaṇḍa*, vol. II, edited and translated by Priyabala Shah [of this passage only] Gaekwad's Oriental Series, no. 137 (Baroda: Oriental Institute, 1961), p. 3.

6. Ananda Coomaraswamy, introduction to Russell Meriweather Hughes, *The Gesture Language of Hindu Dance* (New York: B. Blom, 1941), p. 5.

7. Selection of these particular examples was occasioned by venue. The paper was prepared for delivery at the Minneapolis Institute of Arts, which owns a copy of Rodin's sculpture, as well as a Vijayanagar period image of Pārvatī.

8. Cf. King Nebuchadnezzar's dream of an image composed of progressively baser materials, from head of gold to feet of iron and clay: *Daniel* 2: 31-45.

9. Robert Rosenblum and H.W. Janson, *19th-Century Art* (New York: Harry N. Abrams, 1984), p. 477.

10. *Saundaryalaharī*, vv. 79, 80.

11. This generalization is based upon a survey of the relevant examples in P.R. Srinivasan, *Bronzes of South India* (Madras: Bulletin of the Madras Government Museum, n.s. VIII, 1963).

12. In South India, the consorts of all major deities, irrespective of creed, are represented in this manner.

13. C. Sivaramamurti, *South Indian Bronzes* (New Delhi: Lalit Kala Akademi, 1963), p. 29.

14. E.g., Srinivasan, *Bronzes of South India,* Figs. 99, 123, 279.

15. Ibid., Figs. 137, 159, 169, 219.

16. The same logic applies to the much rarer Tripurāntaka (Śiva as Destroyer of the Three Cities) groups (e.g., Srinivasan,*Bronzes of South India,* Figs. 80, 166) in which the consorts' images lean away from Śiva's relatively extended pose.

17. Tender with passion towards Śiva, disdainful of others, wrathful toward Gaṅgā, amazed at the exploits of Giriśa, fear-stricken by Hara's serpents, victorious over the loveliness of the lotus, smiling toward your companions is your glance, O mother, and to me it is full of compassion.

Saundaryalaharī, v. 51; Hema Rajagopalan performed a Bharata Nāṭyam exposition of this passage at the Chicago Cultural Center, August 27, 1984.

18. P.R. Srinivasan, "Evolution of Some Iconographic Concepts," *Transactions of the Archaeological Society of South India*, vols. 4-6 (1958-60), pp. 38, 39.

19. David D. Shulman, *Tamil Temple Myths: Sacrifice and Divine Marriage in the South Indian Śaiva Tradition* (Princeton, New Jersey: Princeton University Press, 1980), pp. 214-219.

20. I.e., dancing with one leg raised; vertical splits; cf. C. Sivaramamurti, *Naṭarāja in Art, Thought and Literature* (New Delhi: National Museum, 1974), p. 152.

21. It was already alluded to in the 7th century by Appar, one of the major Śaiva saints (cf. the collection of their hymns, *Tevāram,* 666: *patikam* 68.8; cited in Shulman, *Tamil Temple Myths,* p. 213).

22. *Mirror of Gesture*, pp. 50, 51.

23. "Not this, not this"; one of the *mahāvākyas* (great sayings) that characterize the Absolute.

24. "Liberation," the dissolution of individualized existence.

25. Recounted by Cekkilar in the *Periyapurāṇam* (early twelfth century) translated by S.S. Pillai, in *Women Saints of East and West,* Sri Sarada Devi [the Holy Mother] Birth Centenary Memorial (London: Ramakrishna Vedānta Centre, 1953), p. 20.

26. Shulman, *Tamil Temple Myths*, p. 22.

27. For another, non-antithetical view, cf. Ananda Coomaraswamy, "Indian Images with Many Arms," in *The Dance of Śiva*, 1918, rev. ed. (New Delhi: Sagar Publications, 1968), pp. 79-84.

28. Herschel Chipp, *Theories of Modern Art* (Berkeley, California: University of California Press, 1968), pp. 223, 224.

29. Cf. Ananda Coomaraswamy, "The Dance of Śiva," in *The Dance of Śiva*, p. 70.

30. *Nāṭyaśāstra of Bharatmuni*, Chapters 1-7, Illustrated; edited by M. Ramakrishna Kavi, Gaekwad's Oriental Series, no. XXXVI (Baroda: Oriental Series, 1950). Translated by Manomohan Ghosh (Calcutta: Royal Asiatic Society, 1950). Fourth chapter translated as *Tāṇḍava Lakṣaṇam, or the Fundamentals of Ancient Hindu Dancing*, by Venkata Narayanaswami Naidu, Srinivasulu Naidu and Venkata Rangayya Pantulu (Madras: G.S. Press, 1936), p.22.

31. Padma Subrahmanyam, *Bharata's Art: Then and Now.* (Bombay: Bhulabhai Memorial Institute, 1979), p.59. For a contrary view, cf. V. Raghavan, ed., *Nṛttaratnāvalī* [of Jayasenapati, fl. 1253] (Madras: Government Oriental Manuscript Library, 1965), p. 87.

32. Coomaraswamy, *The Dance of Śiva*, p. 76; Heinrich Zimmer, *Myths and Symbols in Indian Art and Civilization*, edited by Joseph Campbell (New York: Harper Torchbooks, 1962), pp. 153, 154.

33. *The Sāṅkhyakārikā of Īśvara Kṛṣṇa*, edited and translated by S.S. Suryanarayana Sastri (Madras: University of Madras, 1935); reprinted in Sarvepalli Radhakrishnan and Charles A. Moore, eds., *A Source Book in Indian Philosophy* (Princeton, New Jersey: Princeton University Press, 1957), *kārikā* no. 59, p. 444.

34. E.g.,

> 9. Furthermore, Secret Master, just as there are no sentient beings and no life in space, so likewise, is there no seer. [These things are] due to the delusion of the mind which causes illusions.

10. Furthermore, Secret Master, they [i.e., the products of delusion] are like images of circles produced by a man taking hold of a firebrand and revolving it in space.

From the *Mahāvairocana Sūtra* (ca. sixth century); translated from the Chinese by Minoru Kiyota, in *Tantric Concept of Bodhicitta: A Buddhist Experiential Philosophy* (Madison, Wisconsin: University of Wisconsin Press, 1983), p. 79.

35. IV: 47. As a fire-brand, when set in motion, appears as crooked, etc., so also Consciousness, when set in motion, appears as the perceiver, the perceived, and the like.

IV: 48. As the fire-brand, when not in motion, is free from all appearances and remains changeless, similarly, Consciousness, when not in motion (imaginary action), is free from all appearances and remains changeless.

The Māṇḍūkyopaniṣad with Gauḍapāda's Kārikā and Śaṅkara's Commentary, translated by Swami Nikhilananda, 6th ed. (Mysore: Sri Ramakrishna Ashrama, 1974), pp. 260,261.

36. Kapila Vatsyayan, *Classical Indian Dance in Literature and the Arts*, 2nd ed. (New Delhi: Sangeet Natak Akademi, 1977), p. 27.

37. Robert Sewell, *A Forgotten Empire (Vijayanagar)*, 1900 reprint ed. (New Delhi: National Book Trust, 1970), p. 277.

38. E.g., "Inverted," "Infolded Thigh," "Shouldered Arms," "Half Whirl,": (nos. 2, 3, 9, and 12 respectively); cf. *Tāṇḍava Lakṣaṇam*, pp. 22, 24.

39. Hermann Kulke, *Cidamabarmāhātmya* (Wiesbaden: O. Harrassowitz, 1970), pp. 84-87.

40. From the root *tantu*, "to dance, skip, leap across, jump over, cross, step over, transgress, excel." T. Burrow and M. B. Emeneau, *A Dravidian Etymological Dictitionary*, 2nd ed. (Oxford: Clarendon Press, 1984), p. 274, no. 3158.

41. *Nāṭyaśāstra*, IV: 85; *Tāṇḍava Lakṣaṇam*, p. 27.

42. *Nāṭyaśāstra*, IV: 161; *Tāṇḍava Lakṣaṇam*, p. 46.

43. E.g., Mohan Khokar, *Traditions of Indian Classical Dance* (New Delhi: Clarion Books, 1979), opp. p. 144.

44. Cf. Udai Narain Roy, *Śālabhañjikā (In Art, Philosophy and Literature)* (Allahabad: Lokbharti Publications, 1979).

45. I am grateful to the Canadian dancer Maureen Sanderson for this information. For a published example of the pose, see Gurmeet Thukral and Mohan Khokar, *The Splendours of Indian Dance* (New Delhi: Himalayan Books, 1986), p. 3.

46. Anne-Marie Gaston, *Śiva in Dance, Myth and Iconography* (Delhi: Oxford University Press, 1982), p. 19.

47. Sivaramamurti, *Naṭarāja in Art*, p. 43; *Tāṇḍava Lakṣaṇam*, Plate X, Fig. 15.

48. E.g., depictions of the hunter-saint Kaṇṇapa Nāyaṉār, who proferred his own eyes to a bleeding *mukhaliṅgam*, in Srinivasan, *South Indian Bronzes*, Plate CXVI; cf. Shulman, *Tamil Temple Myths*, pp. 135-137.

49. *Nāṭyaśāstra*, IV: 129; *Tāṇḍava Lakṣaṇam*, p. 38.

50. Gaston, *Śiva in Dance* , p. 1.

51. Padma Subrahmanyam, "Karaṇas in Dance and Sculpture," Ph. D. dissertation (Madras: Annamalai University [ca. 1963]); and *Bharata's art: Then*

and Now. For a photograph of her in a *Viṣṇukrānta*-like pose, see Thukral and Khokar, *The Splendours of Indian Dance*, p. 27.

Bibliography

Bharata Muni, *Nāṭyaśāstra of Bharatmuni*, Chapters 1-7, Illustrated; edited by M. Ramakrishna Kavi, Gaekwad's Oriental Series, no. XXXVI (Baroda: Oriental Series, 1950). Translated by Manomohan Ghosh (Calcutta: Royal Asiatic Society, 1950). Fourth chapter translated as *Tāṇḍava Lakṣaṇam, or the Fundamentals of Ancient Hindu Dancing*, by Venkata Narayanaswami Naidu, Srinivasulu Naidu and Venkata Rangayya Pantulu (Madras: G.S. Press, 1936).

Brown, W. Norman, editor and translator, *The Saundaryalaharī, or Flood of Beauty: Traditionally Ascribed to Śaṅkarācārya* (Cambridge, Massachusetts: Harvard University Press, 1958).

Burrow, T. and M.B. Emeneau, *A Dravidian Etymological Dictionary*, 2nd ed. (Oxford: Clarendon Press, 1984).

Chipp, Herschel. *Theories of Modern Art* (Berkeley, California: University of California Press, 1968).

Coomaraswamy, Ananda, "Introduction," in Russell Meriweather Hughes, *The Gesture Language of Hindu Dance* (New York: B. Blom, 1941).

Coomaraswamy, Ananda, *The Dance of Śiva*, 1918, rev. ed. (New Delhi: Sagar Publications, 1968).

Gaston, Anne-Marie, *Śiva in Dance, Myth and Iconography* (Delhi: Oxford University Press, 1982).

Gopal, Ram, *Indian Dancing* (Bombay: Asian Publishing House, 1951).

Īśvara Kṛṣṇa, *The Sāṅkhyakārikā*, edited and translated by G.G. Suryanarayana Sastri (Madras: University of Madras, 1935); reprinted in Sarvepalli Radhakrishnan and Charles A. Moore, eds., *A Source Book in Indian Philosophy* (Princeton, New Jersey: Princeton University Press, 1957).

Jayasenapati, *Nṛttaratnāvalī*, edited by V. Raghavan (Madras: Government Oriental Manuscript Library, 1965).

Khokar, Mohan, *Traditions of Indian Classical Dance* (New Delhi: Clarion Books, 1979).

Kiyota, Minoru, *Tantric Concept of Bodhicitta: A Buddhist Experiential Philosophy* (Madison, Wisconsin: University of Wisconsin Press, 1983).

Kulke, Hermann. *Cidambaramāhātmya* (Wiesbaden: O. Harrassowitz, 1970).

Nandikeśvara, *The Mirror of Gesture: Being the Abhinaya Darpaṇa of Nandikeśvara*, translated into English by Ananda Coomaraswamy and Gopala Kristnayya Duggirala, 1917 reprint ed. (New Delhi: Munshriam Manoharlal, 1970).

Nikhilananda, Swami, translator, *The Māṇḍūkyopaniṣad With Gauḍapāda's Kārikā and Śaṅkara's Commentary*, 6th ed. (Mysore: Sri Ramakrishna Ashrama, 1974).

Pillai, S.S., *Women Saints of East and West*, Sri Sarada Devi Birth Centenary Memorial (London: Ramakrishna Vedānta Centre, 1953).

Rosenblum, Robert and H.W. Janson, *19th-Century Art* (New York: Harry N. Abrams, 1984).

Roy, Udai Narain, *Śālabhañjikā (In Art, Philosophy and Literature)* (Allahabad: Lokbharti Publications, 1979).

Sewell, Robert, *A Forgotten Empire (Vijayanagar)*,1900 reprint ed. (New Delhi: National Book Trust, 1970).

Shah, Priyabala, editor and translator, *Viṣṇudharmottara Purāṇa, Third Khaṇḍa*, vol. II, Gaekwad's Oriental Series, no. 137 (Baroda: Oriental Institute, 1961).

Shulman, David Dean, *Tamil Temple Myths: Sacrifice and Divine Marriage in the South Indian Śaiva Tradition* (Princeton, New Jersey: Princeton University Press, 1980).

Sivaramamurti, C., *Naṭarāja in Art, Thought and Literature* (New Delhi: National Museum, 1974).

Sivaramamurti, C., *South Indian Bronzes* (New Delhi: Lalit Kala Akademi, 1963).

Srinivasan, P.R., *Bronzes of South India* (Madras: Bulletin of the Madras Government Museum, n.s. VIII, 1963).

Srinivasan, P.R., "Evolution of Some Iconographic Concepts," *Transactions of the Archaeological Society of South India*, vols. 4-6 (1958-60).

Subrahmanyam, Padma, *Bharata's Art: Then and Now*, (Bombay: Bhulabhai Memorial Institute, 1979).

Subrahmanyam, Padma, "Karaṇas in Dance and Sculpture," Ph.D. dissertation (Madras: Annamalai University [ca. 1963]).

Thukral, Gurmeet and Mohan Khokar, *The Splendours of Indian Dance* (New Delhi: Himalayan Books, 1986).

Vatsyayan, Kapila, *Classical Indian Dance in Literature and the Arts,* 2nd ed. (New Delhi: Sangeet Natak Akademi, 1977).

Zimmer, Heinrich, *Myths and Symbols in Indian Art and Civilization*, edited by Joseph Campbell (New York: Harper Torchbooks, 1962).

VI

Dancing "Virgin," Sexual Slave, Divine Courtesan or Celestial Dancer: In Search of the Historic *Devadāsī*

David Kopf

This article raises questions on the cultural meaning and identity of the "notorious" Hindu temple dancers often indecorously referred to as *devadāsīs*, or slaves of God. As a historically verifiable social grouping within a specific religious context, *devadāsīs* are certainly as old as the earliest free standing temples during the Gupta era (mid-first millennium A.D.).[1] Texts and inscriptions suggest that *devadāsīs* were affiliated with temples in most Hindu kingdoms or feudatories throughout the entire medieval period. It should not be surprising that they served in the great temples of Tanjore or Vijyayanagar or in the magnificent structures of Orissa and Khajurāho, but they also seemingly served in Bengal temples during the Sena era (twelfth century).[2] Whatever were their regional variations in role and function, most of them appear to have been among the most learned women in India.[3] And one can hypothesize that for centuries they preserved the subtle, intricate and highly refined Hindu dramatic arts, including music and dance, which they performed with a consummate skill before priests, pilgrims and princes.

In the British period through Post-Independence, the *devadāsī* lost considerable status and prestige, presumably because her life style ran counter to the values of the Westernized Hindu middle class.[4] In 1930, when the American feminist, Katherine Mayo, lashed out against the oppression of Hindu women, *devadāsīs* had already sunk so low in her estimation as to be placed on the same circle of living hell as the Hindu child bride and adolescent widow.[5] Indeed, thanks to persons with views similar to Mayo's, the Bombay Devadāsī Prevention Act was passed in 1934.[6] In recent years, Indian states have passed land reforms which impoverished temples by depriving them of income from tenant farmers and share-croppers. *Devadāsīs* were "laid off" and forced to migrate to cities like Bombay, where they were victimized by pimps and driven into red light districts like Kamathipura.[7]

Not all temples have lost their capacity to maintain *devadāsīs* and somehow the system manages to survive "modern" India. But is it the system which existed centuries ago? One anthropologist has actually studied *devadāsīs* today in a Puri temple.[8] Unfortunately, however, Indian scholars who are busily reconstituting every other facet of the creative Hindu heritage, persistently ignore the history of *devadāsīs*. The very presence of these women seems to be more a cultural embarrassment than a weighty subject worthy of research. Thus, pathetically, the *devadāsīs* find themselves in a state of limbo between a not inglorious past which no one seems willing to recapture, and the present twilight of their agony as common whores.

Though there is no historiography of *devadāsīs*, there are numerous references to them in both primary sources and in scholarly monographs which mention them in juxtaposition to kindred topics. Whether studied for their own sake or not, their historic image is multi-faceted and confusing. In my opinion, what needs to be done, and what I propose to do in this article, is to examine each of the images in light of the historical imagination which produced it and the kinds of evidence presented in support of it. What follows, then, is an analytical survey of *devadāsī* images which I submit as an introduction to a much larger and ambitious historical study.

The *Devadāsī* as Dancing "Virgin": the Fertility Thesis

One explanation for the *devadāsī's* sexually promiscuous role in the temple is that originally she served as a priestess of love in accordance with the accepted belief that she was a surrogate of the earth mother. The prototypal *devadāsī* offered herself to all men but never belonged to any single man. She has been called a sacred harlot because she gave herself in sacred space and in a manner authorized and sanctified by religious dogma and usage. Therefore, rather than being looked upon as a woman of ill repute, she was not only respected but revered for being close to godliness. And in some mysterious way, her sex act was responsible for agricultural abundance and the general well being of the community.[9]

The models for the later *devadāsīs* were the women who served in the so-called love temples of ancient times. In the early religions, or in those untouched by the Judeo-Christian and Islamic traditions, sex and love were an integral part of the sacred customs. Sex was not yet "naughty, dirty, sinful in the eyes of religion nor had the notion of sin become associated with the process of conceiving new human life."[10]

It was natural that women should be priestesses of one sort or another in temples which were largely dedicated to goddesses. And it was natural that the first deities were largely goddesses since there was an obvious connection between fecundity of the soil and human reproduction. Women gave themselves in temples as part of a sacred ritual which they themselves mastered and supervised and which probably had deep roots in pre-civilized tribal religion.[11]

The kind of temple women whom the *devadāsīs* may have represented were the virgins of the classical Mediterranean cultures whose goddess was Aphrodite and her predecessors.[12] Many scholars are now convinced that the holy virgin of classical and preclassical times was not chaste, the sex-denying woman in the manner of the Virgin Mary. On the contrary, she had much sexual experience because she gave herself freely to every man without feeling dependence on any single man who claimed guardianship or custodial authority over her body and behavior.[13] Briffault claims that the word "virgin" originally meant "unwed" and it is not insignificant that in Greece illegitimate children were called *parthenoi*, or virgin born.[14] According to Esther Harding, the conspicuous quality of this kind of woman was that "she was not dependent on the man, she did not cling to him or demand that the relationship should be permanent." "She was," Harding stresses, "still her own mistress, a virgin in the ancient, original meaning of the word."[15]

In Eastern India there are medieval textual sources which suggest that in some cases virgin, sexual pleasure, and sacred love all conformed to the above classical model.[16] There is a virgin goddess in East Bengal and Assam called Kumārī, or virgin, who is a manifestation of Śakti or woman as the source of divine power. As one scholar puts it, "she was her own mistress and by virtue of her independent status created the universe according to her desire." Professor Kakati who has done research on the history of a love goddess in Assam, believes that in the original sense of the Hindu *kumārī*, "virgin" meant something very different from what it means today. In his own words, "a virgin does not convey the modern meaning of chaste, unspotted; it means unwed, unmarried, and thus free from anybody's control."[17]

It is, however, very difficult for conventional Western or Indian scholars to accept the hypothesis that sex and even dance were legitimate duties or functions of a priestess. From their point of view, *devadāsīs* were more likely the Indian counterparts of the Roman vestal virgins. This is an appealing notion because chastity was enjoined upon a selected elite class of priestly women who had tremendous power and prestige. Chastity, here, was not used in a Christian sense since the Roman women remained pure not for ascetic reasons, but to remain free of custodial control by men who could otherwise manipulate the women for political advantage.[18]

Elise Boulding seems to share this viewpoint in her analysis of temple women in ancient Egypt. When these women performed respectable duties, in her opinion, this indicates that the matriarchy was still alive and well. But when women became entertainers in the temple, then this indicated patriarchal use or misuse of women. For example, in the Old Kingdom of Egypt, all twenty-two Neith priesthoods were held by women whose duties were really quite necessary and varied. They mummify bodies, prepare funeral papyri, are mourners, maintain temples, copy manuscripts, provide religious education..." Then, according to Professor Boulding, these women lost their prerogatives and were allowed merely "to sing and dance in temple choirs."[19]

This position is similar to that of Indians today who argue that in earlier times, *devadāsīs* were pure and spiritual -- especially those who served in Śakti temples. In the notorious Yellamma temple in Karnataka, for example, which still conducts a lively trade in buying or selling women as prostitutes, *devadāsīs* are known as *jogtis*, which has come to mean "whores."[20] *Jogti* is from *yoginī* which, according to a temple inscription, refers to a class of nuns or priestesses who were known and respected for their austere lives of prayer and meditation.[21]

The problem is that though the Karnataka temple inscription suggests that these women led severe lives, elsewhere when they are portrayed in sculpture, they resemble dancing virgins in the classical sense more than vestal virgins or even Christian nuns. In Orissa, where Śaktism developed also, there are a number of *yoginī pīṭhas,* or temple shrines dedicated to the supreme power of woman as god. There are on these temples hundreds of figures of *yoginīs* who dance in the company of drummers and other musicians. In the circular cloisters of one temple alone, at Hirapur, there are sixty-four niches, each holding an image of a *yoginī*. The *yoginīs* are not only beautifully ornamented with exquisite jewelry, but they dance wildly enough for one scholar to believe they are experiencing "spiritual ecstasy."[22]

Is dance, then, so alien to the religious spirit? Havelock Ellis, an early twentieth century sex ethnologist, declared that "dancing is a primitive expression alike of religion and of love."[23] For Ellis, "what a man danced, that was his tribe, his social customs, his religion." "A savage does not preach his religion," he went on to say, "he dances it."[24] Ellis believed that dancing was an "essential" ano "fundamental" part of all "undegenerate religion," including early Christianity.[25] He pointed out that Dante "in assigning so large a place to dancing in the *Paradiso*, described dancing as the occupation of the inmates of Heaven, and Christ as the leader of the dance."[26]

In Ellis' view, dancing as an art represented a transformation form its "primary vital joy" in love or "its sacred function in religion," to professionalism.[27] "Dancing," he wrote, "like priesthood, became a profession, and dancers, like priests, formed a caste."[28] Interestingly enough, it is precisely in this context that Ellis places the *devadāsīs*. They are to him, "at once religious and professional dancers." To quote Ellis in full:

> They are married to gods, they are taught dancing by the Brahmans, they figure in religious ceremonies, and their dances represent the life of the god they are married to as well as the emotions of love they experience for him. Yet, at the same time, they also give professional

> performances in the houses of rich private persons who pay for them.[29]

The key to *devadāsī* origins may lie in the fertility beliefs and practices of the pre-Aryan and non-Aryanized agricultural peoples of India. The new scholarship of social realism has certainly treated erotic sculpture in precisely this manner. Devangana Desai, for example, in her book on Indian erotic art from 500 to 1400 A.D., argues that so-called "ritual prostitution" in temples was not originally erotic in purpose but was derived from the "sexual license everywhere in agricultural festivals connected with the planting of seed and the gathering of harvest."[30] She goes on to say that "in accord with the belief that the goddess of fertility must herself be fertile," she was provided with a male partner. The aim of the union was "to promote fruitfulness of the earth, animals, and mankind."[31] The *devadāsīs* were thus wives of the gods or priestesses of the goddess and whenever they copulated with mortals the pair became "surrogates" of the divine couple.[32]

Some anthropologists and historians believe that the tribals today in outlying parts of the subcontinent may represent the pre-Aryanized culture of contemporary Hindus. The Rajbansis are such a tribal group who live in East Bengal, one of the last and least Aryanized areas of India. Their fertility practices are most interesting from the point of view of answering the question about the pre-temple genesis of the *devadāsī* system. One of their oldest and most revealing ceremonies is called Huduma, which is done in the night of the new moon during a period of prolonged drought.

The women take a plough, a winnowing fan and some paddy seed and go to a nearby uncultivated farm where they engage in mock farming. They then take their clothes off, and begin dancing with their hair hanging loose. Still unclothed, they return to the village which has earlier been depopulated of the men who are religiously prohibited from catching glimpses of the naked women. The women continue to dance throughout the night until daybreak.[33]

During the Ita Pūjā which is a related ceremony of the same group of Rajbansis, women perform the crucial religious role, they express it in ritual by dancing, and there is a strong sexual aspect which is only seemingly erotic, but is a reflection of the more pressing need for fecundity and survival. The Ita Pūjā is performed, once more, when there is a new moon. As reported by an anthropologist, "a dark-skinned, only daughter is made to dance in a field to stimulate the dark cloud that brings a heavy shower." According to the same source, "the songs accompanying this ceremony are highly erotic and obscene."[34]

The *Devadāsī* as Sexual Slave: Victim of Paganism or Feudalism?

Probably the oldest surviving perception of the *devadāsī* is that of enslaved object of sensual gratification and perversion. To morally indignant Christians, she appeared with passion-laden eyes dancing seductively before a lifeless idol, a prisoner of sex and a slave to lecherous brahmin priests. Hindu temples were equated with their pagan prototypes in classical times and reminded Christians of orgiastic rites in the Greco-Roman world, of Dionysian maenads and the promiscuous worshippers of Venus, and of the phallic gods such as Priapus. Above all, irate Christians condemned the *devadāsī* system as the product of a religion totally corrupted by a morally debased and cynical priesthood.[35] As one sardonic Anglo-Indian said of the *devadāsī* system, "to make an absurd but realistic comparison, it is as if Dean Inge added a troop of geishas to the choir of St. Paul's to attract worshippers."[36]

Francois Bernier, A Frenchman who traveled through Moghul India between 1656 and 1668, visited the temple of Jagannātha in Puri, Orissa and discovered there that the god was wedded to a large number of beautiful women. It was Bernier's opinion that these *devadāsīs* were given to the god so that he would be pleased and would reciprocate his pleasure by making the year fruitful.[37] Bernier also believed that brahmin priests served as surrogates of Lord Jagannātha in deflowering fresh recruits among the *devadāsīs*. We are told that the young woman awaits god in her room, but is actually ravished by the impostor priest who "enters her bed and enjoys the unsuspecting damsel."[38] Naturally, Bernier describes the chariot-pulling ritual which shocked Europeans because Hindus felt they could achieve salvation by throwing themselves beneath the wheels of the enormous car and being crushed to death. While this goes on, writes Bernier, "the women dance and throw their bodies into indecent and preposterous attitudes which the Brahmans deem quite consistent with the religion of the country."[39]

The Abbe Dubois who was a French Catholic missionary in Tamil Nadu (South India) during the late eighteenth century, also observed *devadāsī* practices first hand in Madras, Mysore and elsewhere. To him, first of all, there was little difference in the way the women were treated in either Śiva or Viṣṇu temples. There was little doubt in Dubois' mind that the women were not so much servants or wives of the god as they were slaves of the temple establishment. In one place, for example, he described how brahmins went about recruiting women for the Veṅkateśvara temple in Karnataka. He wrote that the priests "go into the crowd and pick the most beautiful women, demanding them of their husbands or parents in the name of Vishnu."[40] Then, once the women belonged to the temple, those who are slaves of Viṣṇu "have a Garuda-like bird tattooed on their breasts, while those belonging to Shiva have a lingam tattooed on their thighs."[41]

The Abbe Dubois distinguished between two classes of temple women. The priestesses functioned as wives of Śiva or Viṣṇu, whereas the *devadāsīs* sang and danced for him. Both, according to him, "were equally depraved."[42] The priestesses were debauched by priests rather much as Bernier reported took place at the temple of Puri. "We know," writes Dubois, "that these worthy *gurus* enjoy the privilege of representing in everything the gods whose ministers they are."[43] As for the *devadāsīs*, their duties consisted of dancing and singing in the temple each morning and evening and also at public festivals from time to time. To Dubois, their dance gestures were highly obscene and totally inappropriate for promoting any kind of spiritual purpose. In fact, they were educated to be endowed with qualities which were more befitting the prostitute than a woman dedicated to a religious life. It was his impression that "during the intervals of the various ceremonies" *devadāsīs* were involved in "more shameful practices." Thus, among Hindus, "even sacred temples were converted into mere brothels."[44]

Interestingly enough, the image of *devadāsīs*, as depicted in the work of contemporary Marxist and other social realist historians in India, is strikingly similar to that of the European Christians. Both expose the hypocrisies of the medieval Hindu establishment and both condemn the exploitation and victimization of women in the most indignant terms. The main difference is that Christians blame sexual slavery on Hindu paganism, whereas Hindu social realists tend to indict a feudal class or an aristocratic elite. Professor Narendra Nath Bhattacharyya, a social realist, blames patriarchal institutions as well as feudalism. By equating Śaktism with the indigenous faith of the Hindu masses, Bhattacharyya has traced many of the abuses of the Hindu social order back to the Aryan imposition of a patriarchal system upon the existing system of mother worship and mother right.[45]

Social realists in India also tend to view the earlier *devadāsīs* in a more positive light as women selected by the community to sacrifice their virtue for the social good. We have already noted that Devangana Desai is an advocate of the fertility thesis and has sought to prove that "the essential idea behind the performance of the sexual act in and around the holy shrine is that it promotes all natural fruitfulness and the general welfare of the community."[46] Even so-called "obscene sculpture" in the very same temples where *devadāsīs* carried on their sacred duties, "expressed the same purpose as agrarian rituals," for both, according to Desai, "functioned to stimulate the generative powers of nature."[47]

This was probably true in North India until approximately 900 A.D. Desai's analysis of changing styles in maithuna (sculpture of coital poses) has convinced her that the art form lost its popular simplicity and became an ostentatious display of orgiastic art representing, sociologically, the interests and pleasure of the dominant feudal class.[48] Such temples as those in Tanjore or Khajurāho, for example, had lost their "original association with fertility, their original meaning, and became the means of pleasure garbed in the form of worship."[49] In the same period, and as part of the same process, the *devadāsīs*, whose numbers increased greatly, lost their sacred function as servants of god and the people, and became prostitutes for the pleasure of the elite.[50]

Devangana Desai takes a rather dim view of the courtly elite who misused *devadāsīs* as courtesans with their customary class callousness and indifference to religious feeling and moral compassion. She reminds us that some rulers were the chief donors of temples over which they asserted control and dictated policy in a manner designed to transform the sacred character of the institutions.[51] "Too often," writes Desai, "the atmosphere of a medieval temple was a breeding ground for luxurious living and degenerate sex practices."[52]

To support her argument, Desai cites a poem by a chief minister of the Kashmiri king Jayāpīḍa (779-813), in which is described a performance of a Harṣa play, *Ratnāvalī*, in a Śiva temple. Not only is the heroine of the play acted by a *devadāsī*, but the purpose of giving the performance is to seduce the prince of a nearby state. Dāmodaragupta, the author of the poem, leaves little doubt in the mind of the reader that the temple had much less to do with religious devotion than with promoting promiscuous sex.[53] Temples were popular because *devadāsīs* were sought by royal paramours, pilgrims and "fake *sādhus*."[54] Bilhaṇa, another Kashmiri poet, wrote about *devadāsīs* that they were beautiful, that they "glorified sex" and that they were superb actresses. And not too infrequently, he added, "kings would take *devadāsīs* as concubines into the royal seraglio."[55]

The *Devadāsī* as Divine Courtesan: The Hindu Erotic Tradition, Sacred and Profane

At least one Indian scholar has argued, not unconvincingly, that the pleasures of sex and love are not peripheral themes in Indian civilization, but are the life-blood of the efflorescence of all Indian art and culture and have come to determine the typically Indian attitude to life and the world.[56]

In 1966, Kanwar Lal contemplated a five-volume work on "India's attitude to love and passion."[57] For Lal, the true dialectic throughout the ages in Hindu civilization has been the intense struggle between the devotees of Lord Kāma (Eros) who worship the body, beauty and love for women, as against the devotees of sterile other-worldliness who deny life, love and the aesthetic sensibility.[58] Perhaps no other Indian male has so effectively exposed the misogyny underlying patriarchal Indian thought, both Hindu and Buddhist. The *sine qua non* of the Hindu erotic tradition was the living manifestation of the divine woman, Śakti: alluring, cultivated, loving, and tender, with an acute intellect, poetic sense and superb mastery of song and dance.[59]

The kind of woman Lal and others seem to have in mind as their ideal is the courtesan. Though the term itself was invented in sixteenth century Europe to depict a much sought after courtly woman of charm, intellect and easy virtue,[60] her type existed in all classical Eurasian civilizations from Greece to China. In India, she appeared in all the major literary works, from the scriptural Vedas to the poems and plays of the Gupta and post-Gupta eras. She was the proverbial other woman in courtly society among aristocrats and other elites. One of the most common themes in the Hindu classics was the ruination of kings, princes, merchants, priests, mystics and even sages, by courtesans. If the famous erotic classic, the *Kāma Sūtra*, were dedicated to a single class of women, it would surely not be the legal wives or the sexual slaves (common prostitutes), but the courtesans who were masters of the sixty-four arts of which, interestingly enough, eight were devoted to music and dance.[61]

According to S.K De, a historian of Sanskrit literature, the courtesan was often portrayed as a heroine who "occupied an important position in society" because she had "skill and charm, wealth and power as well as literary and artistic taste."[62] Van Buitenen translated one such Sanskrit play, *The Little Clay Cart,* which is about one such courtesan, Vasantasenā, whom he describes in the following way:

> She was a free woman walking and dancing with the self-assurance of the courtesan, darling of the sophisticated

> town, with almost every gesture and word excitingly violating all the proper ways for a matron to behave -- a woman watched and admired like sin itself...[63]

A hypothesis worth considering is that with the decline and fall of classical Sanskritic civilization, the courtesan tradition was maintained by the introduction of the *devadāsīs* into the temples. Thus, the beautiful women sculptured on medieval temples and shrines along with the images of copulating couples, were not created merely to frighten evil spirits away or to increase last year's yield of crops.

In fact, many art historians deny any connection between the sculptured beauties and primitive fertility rites, arguing, instead, that they are derivatives of the classical tradition, most likely artistic renditions of India's celestial courtesans known as *apsarases*. These beautiful, nymph-like creatures who may have been the true prototypes of the *devadāsīs*, were perhaps the most intriguing female inventions of the Indo-European mind in India. They were depicted in classical literature as perfect women, or divine courtesans, and even sang and danced at religious festivals rather much as did the *devadāsīs*.[64]

The *apsarases* appeared in the *Atharvaveda* as courtesans of the gods, who were not only enchantingly beautiful, but were superb dancers and musicians.[65] In the *Mahābhārata*, they achieved a kind of individuation, especially when *asparases* such as Ghṛtācī, Menakā, Urvaśī, Miśrakeśī and others danced before Arjuna.[66] Urvaśī tried to seduce Arjuna, but failed.[67] The earliest known elaborate reference to the dance form in which Kṛṣṇa interacted erotically with the *gopīs* is found in the *Harivaṃśa*. The *apsarases* took the parts of the *gopīs* while Arjuna played Kṛṣṇa.[68]

The *apsaras* seemed to function as the pure, almost Platonic idea of the courtesan in Sanskrit literature. She may have been a product of the imagination, generated by aristocrats with refined erotic sensibilities who needed continual sensual arousal and passionate love. Even the myth of creation surrounding the *apsaras* recalls the Aphrodite-Venus birth scene. The sea of milk was churned to extract *amṛta*, a nectar-like substance of the gods, and in the process, there arose out of the foam a troop of celestial nymphs.

Quite possibly, in the medieval period when new religious currents swept Hinduism and the temple arose as a critical institution, sacred *devadāsīs* replaced secular courtesans as the new earthly manifestation of the divine *apsarases*.[69] Just about this time the confusion began--at least in the minds of later scholars--between the erotic as profane and as spiritual. At least in eastern India, we are on the eve of the period which produced that delicious ambiguity known as erotic mysticism. In Bengali Sahajiyā, for example, Dimock has explored precisely this kind of ambiguity in terms of a duality between *kāma*, or lust, and *prema*, or spiritual love, which was nevertheless rooted in the physical act of sex.[70]

The evidence in extant medieval literature suggests that *devadāsīs* continued the classical courtesan tradition on the one hand, and became the focal point for the new erotic mysticism on the other. There are, of course, other possibilities as well, indicating a good deal more pluralism in medieval India than scholars are willing to admit. In the first place, the earlier princely class did not disappear, nor did their amatory pursuits and recreational patterns. Thus, *devadāsīs* performed the courtesan role for the aristocrats in the court when they were not performing their sacred role before the deitites in the temple. But, in fact, as reported in some literature, the temple became hardly distinguishable from the palace and in Kashmir, evidently, temples were often thinly-disguised pleasure palaces.[71]

No doubt, as irate Christians and social realists contend, women were exploited by the princely elite as sexual slaves. But other scholars have stressed the momentous religious changes which swept over India throughout the Hindu Middle Ages, in which erotic mysticism played an important part. I have already noted the importance of Śaktism or the worship of woman as the supreme god. And there was Tantrism, whether of the left- or right-hand variety, which deeply influenced religion and society.[72] Mircea Eliade has stated unequivocally that Tantrism was the most momentous single religious current in the Hindu Middle Ages. Not only did its ideas radically change every strata of Indian society, but in a "comparatively short time, Indian philosophy, mysticism, ritual, ethics, iconography, and even literature are influenced by Tantrism."[73] As a "pan-Indian movement," Eliade concluded, "it is assimilated by all the great Indian religions and by all the 'sectarian' schools."[74]

If *yoga* is *bhoga* (sexual bliss), as scholars of Tantric cults have been telling us since the 1960s, some of the erotic temples, at least, were something more than training and recruiting centers for exceptional women to service the elite. Some very sensitive and sophisticated Westerners such as Herbert Guenther and Alan Watts saw in Tantric ideology and practice something positive in the way sex and religion were fused to produce a higher awareness of Being. As Watts put it, "religion without sex is a rattling skeleton and sex without religion is a mass of mush."[75] Guenther spelled out the process in this way:

> We begin with sex which quite literally is the beginning of ourselves, but sex is not a mere manipulation of organs; it generates an awareness of the value of being. What on the previous level was a cold abstraction becomes now a living symbol pointing to the source, Being-as-such, and through its experience we return to the world differently.[76]

The Important thing emphasized by scholars like Watts and Guenther was that we had to stop treating women as sexual objects, depersonalized and faceless. Watts was certainly emphatic about the kind of sex of which he did not approve, such as the "wham-bam-thank-you-ma'am style of intercourse which generally prevailed through much of the world and in which the purpose was merely the attainment of male orgasm."[77] Guenther is no less emphatic about the shortcomings of Western sexual attitudes which are "inextricably tied up with the contempt for and fear of the body."[78] The following quotation by Guenther contains a most interesting indictment of Western sexuality by a convert to Tantric Buddhism:

> The official attitude has been and is in favour of continence, abstinence, and asceticism having their root in fear, and while contempt might assist the official

> attitude, it more often has been in opposition of it...Libertinism did not appear under the auspices of communion and joy, but under those of arrogance and contempt. To suffer from an obsessive fear of the body is perhaps not so different from a compulsive addiction to sex, be these addicts virility-provers or seductiveness-provers. The important point to note is that in all these cases sex is confined to only one dimension, sensual pleasure and exploitation, but the aesthetic experience of joy and through it the enrichment of one's Being is missed...[79]

Guenther's notion of the role of woman in awakening the proper sexual attitude for spiritual liberation seems to be taken from Tantrism and was one of the most important ideas to permeate erotic mysticism in medieval India. "Conventional masculinity," to Guenther, made any sacred unity of the sexes impossible. It generated "selfishness that does not allow a man to know a woman at all."[80] It thrived on the "degradation of the female sex" which prohibited any true emotional contact and reduced sex "to brutal dominance."[81] The antidote to such masculinization which Śākto-Tantrism provided, was for a man to join "the cult of woman...and to take her as a guide in the profound drama of integration."[82]

It is no wonder that when Watts went to Konārak and saw the *devadāsīs* immortalized in art either as objects of solitary beauty or in erotic postures with others, he proclaimed that the pornography which the Victorians and other puritans believed they had beheld, was not real, but was "only in the eyes of people with dirty minds." "The faces are innocent of the leer," wrote Watts, "which always masks shame and guilt at finding 'pleasure in filth.'"[83]

The identification of the erotic with the spiritual in a pure and undefiling way was the underlying theme in tales of brahmins who fell in love with *devadāsīs* or other temple women. In the Telugu region, there is the story of a brahmin named Kṣetrajña who was a poet and a scholar of Telugu and Sanskrāit literature, music and dance. He fell in love with a *devadāsī* from his village who inspired him to compose devotional songs to her god, Veṇugopālaswamy. Then, he joined a group of Kucipuḍi dancers for whom he composed songs. Significantly, Kṣetrajña is known in Telugu literature for his intense theism and, at the same time, he is popular for the delicate erotic quality of his poetry.[84]

In the tradition of the Kṛṣṇa-Rādhā erotic interplay, the most famous brahmin poet in all India was the twelfth century Jayadeva who composed the great sacred epic of Vaiṣṇavas, the *Gīta Govinda*, for his *devadāsī* wife at the Jagannātha temple in Puri.[85] It is noteworthy about the ambiguities of the flesh and spirit in Hinduism, that Jayadeva, author of a book which, many believe, focuses exclusively on physical passion, should be claimed as the favorite son of several Indian states from Bengal to Kerala.[86]

A later Bengali brahmin poet in the tradition of Jayadeva was Caṇḍīdāsa. In the past, he was believed to have been one person who lived in the fifteenth century, but today scholars are inclined to believe there were many persons who used his name since the fifteenth century and then imitated his style and technique.[87] The consensus among scholars is that the original Caṇḍīdāsa fell in love with a temple servant of a local female love deity names Vāsulī Devī, presumably a Hindu variant of a Buddhist Tantric goddess. Rāmī, his beloved, may or may not have been a *devadāsī*, but legend has it that like *devadāsīs* today, she was probably a *Harijan*. And true to the Śākto-Tantric spirit which evidently permeated the Sahajiyā movement, Caṇḍīdāsa revered her as an embodiment of Śakti at the same time that he ignored caste distinction. Whether true or not, his views did not sit well with his brahmin peers who outcasted him.[88]

Caṇḍīdāsa was an erotic mystic of the Tantricized Sahajiyā tradition whose poetry reflects that exquisite tension between the initial sexual impulse and pure undefiled love.[89] The moral objective of Caṇḍīdāsa's spiritual quest seemed almost Christian at times, except for his intense reverence for woman and his belief that one can be trained in being involved sexually without experiencing carnal desire. Perhaps no other medieval Hindu poet has so eloquently defended the moral value of sanctified sex at the same time he warned devotees how hard it was to travel the path between lust for a woman and salvation achieved through a woman's embrace. "To be a true lover," Caṇḍīdāsa wrote, "one must be able to make a frog dance in the mouth of a snake,"[90] or "dangle a mountain with a cotton thread," or "imprison an elephant in a cobweb."[91] The tone and spirit of the religion of love was also contained in the goddess Vāsulī's command to Caṇḍīdāsa:

> Conquering the temptation of the senses, you must love this woman. No god can offer you what this woman is able to in terms of the purity of heart.[92]

The Fifth Veda and the *Devadāsī* as Celestial Dancer: Orientalism, Brahmanism and the Hindu Renaissance

The challenge to what was largely a foreign attack on Hinduism as a "corrupt" socio-religious system came from British officials in India early in the nineteenth century known as Orientalists. I have written elsewhere about the amateur philologists, archeologists, historians, philosophers and humanists who rediscovered the pre-medieval Hindu tradition, defended it as a golden age, then explained the subsequent corruption as a dark age period of excrescences on the authentic Brahmanic heritage.[93] For the most part, the wonder that was classical India emerged from texts which the Orientalists originally translated and published for Western scholarly consumption. In Europe, the Orientalist discoveries had so profound an effect that according to one scholar it led to a second European renaissance.[94]

In the twentieth century Orientalism lost its purely classical identification and many scholars, beginning with John Woodroffe, found the Hindu dark ages lighter and brighter than their predecessors had cared to admit. Working with a medieval "excrescence" known as Śākto-Tantrism, Woodroffe restored its respectability among brahmins by proving that in its purest form it in no way violated the classical principles of Brahmanism.[95] By removing Śākto-Tantrism from its orgiastic setting, and spiritually elevating the ritual through which fish, meat, wine and sex became sublimated and symbolic attributes of a higher meaning, Woodroffe provided a paradigm of those determined to counter the Christian conception of lecherous old brahmins corrupting themselves and the beautiful young maidens they sought.[96]

Scholars such as Coomaraswamy, Eliade, Zimmer, S.B. Dasgupta and Gopinath Kaviraj owe much to Woodroffe. These Neo-Orientalists have gone to great lengths to demonstrate that the Brahmanic legacy could not be easily dismissed as a facade for licentiousness. Superficial observers, they argued, especially Westerncentric Hinduphobes, totally misread what was in fact a tradition that carried the religious spirit and aesthetic sensibility to heights no other civilization has achieved.[97]

In this way, many once disreputable cults and movements lost their folk connection or revolutionary origins and with the help of the orthodox establishment, ascended Brahmanical Olympian heights. With reference to *devadāsīs*, it is the dance which has only recently begun to be reevaluated and, in the process, the sexual slave, sacred harlot, or divine courtesan is gradually finding redemption. The fact is that the contemporary aura surrounding what is called Indian classical dance is indeed a revolutionary concept because dance in India was, and still is in some quarters, associated with erotic stimulation and prostitution.[98]

Nevertheless, scholars have turned to the history of dance partly out of regional pride, and partly out of a renaissance pride in the revival of clasical art and literature. Bharata's *Nāṭyaśāstra*, for example, which is an ancient text for the classical Hindu dance and drama, has won recognition, even veneration, as a kind of fifth Veda of the performing arts.[99] Today, four regional dances of India are recognized as classical: Kathak (Rajasthan and West India), Bharata

Nāṭyam (Tamil Nadu), Odissi (Orissa), and Maṇipurī (Assam, Bengal). This is no mean achievement when it is considered that these dances traditionally evoked sexual feeling by means of costume, posture and movement. Moreover, a dance like Kathak has been, since the Moghul period, openly and directly associated with sensuality.[100]

But, generally, scholars seem to be in the process of transforming the image of these regional dances and with them the image of the *devadāsīs*. Odissi is a case in point. In Orissa, the dance developed within the temple under the guidance of priestly *gurus*. Thus, historians of dance remind us, dance was devised to serve god and its passion was reserved for achieving spiritual ecstasy.[101] But even long before the medieval period when temples became the pivot of Hindu life, dance was associated with religion and morality. Bharata's myth on the origin of dance is usually offered as evidence to support this point. Indra approached Brahmā to complain that the people had turned to evil ways. After considerable meditation, Brahmā invented dance and drama as a fifth Veda for those who could not study the scriptures or appreciate them intellectually. These arts would teach the spiritual and moral laws directly by appealing to the senses.[102]

Devadāsīs were an integral part of the new Hindu system with its stress on favoring patronage of the temple and its activities. The distinctly medieval scriptures known as Purāṇas not only guaranteed salvation to those who patronized temples, but urged the practice of dedicating dancing girls to the deities as a sure way of winning heaven.[103] The earliest inscription in Orissa which connects the consecration of a temple with the dedication of *davadāsīs* dates back to the Śiva temple of Brahmeswar by the last king of the Kesari dynasty in the tenth century.[104] There are a series of such inscriptions right through to the Gajapati period of the sixteenth century.[105]

It has not been easy to transform the image of the Odissi dance tradition in Orissa. The numerous references to sacred prostitution at the Jagannātha temple in Puri cannot be dismissed easily. The highly publicized "love temple" at Konārak with its sculptured display of frankly erotic art is probably the most frequented tourist attraction in Orissa. Moreover, the most common theme of Odissi dance is the highly eroticized love play of Kṛṣṇa and Rādhā as described in the *Gīta Govinda*. Nevertheless, attempts have been made to suggest that all this sex in sacred places is not what it appears to be.[106]

In the first place, the *devadāsīs* of the temple in Puri, known as *māhārīs*, were, we are now told, originally pure and chaste servants of the Lord Jagannātha.[107] Muslim conquest was later responsible for the moral degeneration of the *māhārīs*.[108]

Renaissance scholars now maintain that dancing among Hindus was never meant for any other purpose but spiritual devotion. Before the system was corrupted, it was danced by those women who were worthy of doing so. Odissi dance could not have been the monopoly of female sexual slaves, it is argued, since there were cases of royal women being trained in the art. Princess Candrikā, for one, daughter of Anaṅgabhīmadevā, was an accomplished dancer and singer. She was also an ardent devotee of Viṣṇu to whom she built her own temple, the Ananta Vāsudeva, in Bhubaneswar.[109]

The erotic exploits of Rādhā and Kṛṣṇa in Vṛndāvana forest present no special problem for most Indian scholars since it has become long fashionable for Vaiṣṇava devotees to defend the *Gīta Govinda* as a spiritual allegory. In Orissa, however, there is the additional problem about the author of the great poem, Jayadeva, whom Oriya scholars hold up as a regional hero.[110] For sometime, the established view was that Jayadeva was a Bengali born in the Birbhum district, won fame as a poet and became one of the "five gems" in the court of Lakṣmaṇa Sena, the "Vikramāditya of Bengal" (1179-1205).[111]

In Orissa, it is believed that Jayadeva was born in their region and that he composed his classic not for a royal patron, but for the temple of Jagannātha "as an essential part of the ritual services...."[112] The *Gīta Govinda* was never intended to be secular or pornographic. Jayadeva has been misunderstood. He was "a learned poet of spiritual devotion." His *Gīta* was a "hymn to be sung and danced before the god."[113]

Conclusion

Not all Hindus have accepted the new morality of the Hindu Renaissance. As we have seen, not all Indian scholars seem comfortable with the de-eroticized self-view of Hindu art and civilization. P.V. Subramaniam, the dance critic, has been among those who have spoken out against the pious ones who erroneously see Jayadeva as "religious and celestial" and his poem as unequivocally allegorical.[114] Prudishness, he believes, has even infected the Odissi dancers of the present generation, who have totally ignored the original uninhibited eroticism of the *Gīta Govinda*.

That *devadāsīs* should come under attack by reformers as an erotic object should not be difficult to understand. They are certainly expendable. But, significantly enough, the dance traditions which *devadāsīs* performed for centuries and centuries as a sacred duty, have not only been preserved, but have been revitalized and modernized as part of the Hindu Renaissance. The dances have been removed from the temple precinct to the concert hall, where a new class of professionals carry on an old sacred tradition in a secular setting, although much of the music and poetical texts for individual dance items still bear the mark of their former religious milieu. And today, in India, and wherever Hindus have settled abroad, the successors of the *devadāsīs* are the little girls from respectable upper and middle class Hindu families who study classical Indian dance.

Notes

1. The tendency today is to talk about the origins of the *devadāsī* system in historical sections of books on Indian prostitution. Perhaps the earliest reference to these women is in Kālidāsa (third century A.D.), who mentions that they were attached to the Mahākāla temple in Ujjain. See V. Agnihotri, *Fallen Women* (Kanpur: Maharaja, n.d.), p.3. By the fourth century A.D., the custom of dedicating women to temples may have already been in vogue in many parts of India, though *devadāsīs* then may have simply "given themselves to a life of religious service and austerities." See S.D. Punekar, *A Study of Prostitutes in Bombay* (Bombay: Lalvani Publishing House, 1967), p.3. See also, M.R. Rao, *The Prostitutes of Hyderabad* (Hyderabad: Association for Moral and Social Hygiene in India, n.d.), p. 7.

2. There are many kinds of sources which testify to the presence of *devadāsīs* from one end of India to the other. There is a Chinese Buddhist pilgrim report on *devadāsīs* in Multan City in the seventh century. Marco Polo was among the earliest Europeans to observe *devadāsīs* when they traveled through the Malabar coast in 1290. In 1522, a Portuguese traveler named Paes visited Vijayanagar in Andhra and reported that *devadāsīs* treated the god Viṭṭhalasvāmi like a husband by feeding him, dancing before him, and catering to his every need. There are numerous references to the system in Muslim accounts such as the report of Mahmud of Ghazni's conquest of the temple of Somnāth in Gujurat in 1094; among the spoils captured were 300 musicians and 500 dancing girls who, together with innumerable brahmins, were supported by 10,000 villages. Literary texts referred to later in this article and many inscriptions offer evidence of *devadāsīs* in Bengal, Kashmir, Orissa, and Tamil Nadu.

3. This is often grudgingly admitted by modern puritanical Hindu academics who are inclined to dismiss the period for its "very low standard of sexual morality." See comments and footnote 3 in R.C. Majumdar, "Medieval Bengali Society," in R.C. Majumdar, ed., *The History of Bengal: Hindu Period* (Dacca: University of Dacca, 1943), p. 619.

4. This is beautifully illustrated in South India with the near death of Bharata Nāṭyam as a classical dance form in the late nineteenth century. Apparently, the dance was totally boycotted by society for 50 years or until 1925 because of its association with *devadāsīs*. Though the *devadāsīs* have disappeared since then in Tamil Nadu, the dance has not only been revived but has undergone a renaissance. See E. Bhavnani, *The Dance In India* (Bombay: D.B. Taraporevala Sons & Co. Private Ltd., 1979), p. 29.

5. For an excellent discussion of Mayo in the context of Indian women reformers in the late 1920s and early 1930s, see G. Forbes, "Inside Pushing Back the Walls: A study of the Indian Women's Movement" (unpublished manuscript), Chapter VII, pp. 9-11.

6. For a good background to this act and to others which preceded it, see H.R. Travedi, *Scheduled Caste Women: Studies in Exploitation* (Delhi: Concept Publishing Company, 1977), pp. 1-8.

---

7. Of 350 common prostitutes from Kamathipura interviewed in the early 1960s, 32.29% were former *devadāsīs*. Cf. Punekar, *A Study of Prostitutes in Bombay*, pp. 12-13. Punekar also provides a brief history of Kamathipura in pp. 8-11.

8. F.A. Marglin, *Wives of the God-King: The Rituals of the Devadasis of Puri* (Delhi: Oxford University Press, 1985).

9. The type of woman referred to in the above paragraph has been generalized about in a great variety of studies dealing with ancient religion, mythology, the origins of consciousness, prostitution, venereal disease, agriculture and the history of sacred sexuality during the alleged pre-patriarchal era when woman was god. Seen from an equally diverse array of disciplinary orientations, from Jungian psychoanalysis to feminist scholarship, these women have been called priestesses of love, sacred harlots, hierodules, celestial sluts and virgins. They served the goddess Ishtar, her many variations in West Asia and Aphrodite in Greece.

10. M. Stone, *When God Was A Woman* (New York: Harcourt, Brace, Jovanovich, 1978), p. 155.

11. See chapter on "Sacred Sex Customs" in ibid., pp. 153-199..

12. See discussion on the origins of Aphrodite in P. Friedrich, *The Meaning of Aphrodite* (Chicago, Illinois: University of Chicago Press, 1978), pp. 9-54.

13. For a succinct depiction of the virgin archetype, see N. Hall, *The Moon and the Virgin* (New York: Harper & Row, 1980), pp. 11-12.

14. R. Briffault, *The Mothers* (New York: Macmillan Company, 1927), vol. III, p. 18. See also the semantic discussion of "parthenos" in Friedrich, *The Meaning of Aphrodite*, p. 86.

15. M.E. Harding, *Woman's Mysteries, Ancient and Modern* (New York: Harper & Row, 1976), pp. 103-104.

16. I refer here to the *Kālikā Purāṇa, Yoginī Tantra* and *Tripurā Rahasya*. All three sources deal in part with the worship of Tripura as a virgin goddess. The Tripurā Sundarī, or beautiful goddess is very much like Aphrodite because of her power which she derives from beauty and sensuality.

17. B.K. Kakati, *The Mother Goddess Kāmākhyā* (Gauhati, Assam: K.C. Pal, 1967), p. 50.

18. E. Boulding, *The Underside of History* (Boulder, Colorado: Westview Press, 1976), pp. 150-51.

19. Ibid., p. 185.

20. Punekar, *A Study of Prostitutes in Bombay*, p. 205.

21. Ibid.

22. D.N. Patnaik, *Odissi Dance* (Bhubaneswar: Orissa Sangeet Natak Akademi, 1971), p. 12.

23. H. Ellis, *The Dance of Life* (New York: Modern Library, 1929), p. 35.

24. Ibid., p. 36.

25. Ibid., p. 40.

26. Ibid., p.41.

27. Ibid., p. 49.

28. Ibid.

29. Ibid.

30. D. Desai, *Erotic Sculpture of India: A Socio-Cultural Study* (New Delhi: Tata McGraw-Hill Publishing Co., 1975), p. 90.
31. Ibid.
32. Ibid., p. 107.
33. A. Sattar, *In The Sylvan Shadows* (Dacca: Saquib Brothers, 1971), p. 108.
34. Ibid., p. 109.
35. For a comprehensive view of the Christian anti-Hindu movement in British India during the early nineteenth century which underlay British attitudes to *devadāsīs*, see D. Kopf, *British Orientalism and the Bengal Renaissance* (Berkeley, California: University of California Press, 1969), pp. 119-144. See also E.A. Payne, *The Śāktas* (Oxford: Oxford University Press, 1933) and M. Monier-Williams, *Hinduism* (London: Society for Promoting Christian Knowledge, 1925).
36. Sir G. Macmunn, *The Religions and Hidden Cults of India* (Delhi: Oriental Publishers, 1975), p. 103.
37. F. Bernier. *Travels in the Mogul Empire*, translated by A. Constable (Oxford: Oxford University Press, 1934), p. 305.
38. Ibid.
39. Ibid.,p. 306.
40. Abbe J.A. Dubois, *Hindu Manners, Customs and Ceremonies*, translated by H.K. Beauchamp (Oxford: Clarendon Press, 1906), p. 601.
41. Ibid., p. 602.
42. Ibid., p. 133.
43. Ibid.
44. Ibid., p. 585.
45. For a good example of this, see N.N. Bhattacharyya, *The Indian Mother Goddess* (New Delhi: Manohar, 1977), pp. 1-34, 253-277.
46. Desai, *Erotic Sculpture of India*, p. 106.
47. Ibid., p. 97.
48. Ibid., p. 147.
49. Ibid., p. 161.
50. Ibid., p. 172.
51. Ibid., pp. 159-162.
52. Ibid., p. 160.
53. Ibid., p. 162.
54. Ibid.
55. Ibid.
56. See K. Lal, *The Cult of Desire* (Delhi: Asia Press, 1966), pp. 1-7.
57. Besides *The Cult of Desire*, Lal published *The Religion of Love* (Delhi: Arts & Letters, 1971) and *Apsaras of Khajurāho* (Delhi: Asia Press, 1966). Walter Spink, the American, wrote a comparative study of Western alienation and Indian eroticism in *The Axis of Eros* (New York: Penguin Books, 1973). There are many books of this kind which see Indian culture as basically erotic.
58. This is the theme of *The Cult of Desire*.
59. Lal's view of women can be found in the sections on Rādhā in *The Religion of Love* and *Apsaras of Khajurāho*.

60. "Courtesan" evidently is related to "courtier" and the background for it is an Italian Renaissance conception of courtly love in the atmosphere of the salon. A brief description of the historical situation appears in V. Bullough and B. Bullough, *An Illustrated Social History of Prostitution* (New York: Crown Publishers, Inc., 1978), pp. 134-136.
61. See Part VI, "On Courtesans and Their Way of Life," in Vatsyayana, *Kāma Sūtra*, translated by S.C. Upadhyaya (Bombay: Taraporevala Sons & Co., 1970), pp. 205-231.
62. S.K. De, *Ancient Indian Erotics and Erotic Literature* (Calcutta: Firma K.L. Mukhopadhyay, 1959), p. 79.
63. J.A.B. Van Buitenen, *Two Plays of Ancient India* (New York: Columbia University Press, 1968), p. 37.
64. K. Vatsyayan, *Classical Indian Dance in Literature and the Arts* (New Delhi: Sangeet Natak Akademi, 1968), p. 169.
65. Ibid., p. 191.
66. Ibid., p. 192.
67. Ibid., pp. 194-195.
68. Lal, *Apsaras of Khajurāho*, p. 1.
69. Ibid., p. 3.
70. E.C. Dimock, *The Place of the Hidden Moon* (Chicago, Illinois: University of Chicago Press, 1966), pp. 161-164.
71. That this was happening throughout India is the argument of N.N. Bhattacharyya in *History of Indian Erotic Literature* (New Delhi: Munshiram Manoharlal Publishers Pvt. Ltd., 1975), pp. 26-30; Desai, *Erotic Sculpture of India*, p. 163.
72. For an excellent introduction to Tantrism, see N.N. Bhattacharyya, *History of the Tantric Religion* (New Delhi: Manohar, 1982).
73. M. Eliade, *Yoga: Immortality and Freedom*, translated by W.R. Trask (New York: Pantheon Books, 1958), p. 200.
74. Ibid.
75. A. Watts, *Erotic Spirituality* (New York: Macmillan Company, 1971), p. 80.
76. H. V. Guenther, *The Tantric View of Life* (London: Shambhala, 1976), p. 76.
77. Watts, op. cit., p. 74.
78. Guenther, op. cit., p. 7.
79. Ibid., p. 65.
80. H. V. Guenther, *Yuganaddha: The Tantric View of Life* (Varanasi: Chowkhamba Sanskrit Series, 1952), p. 65.
81. Ibid., p. 68.
82. Ibid., p. 72.
83. Watts, op. cit., p. 58.
84. M.A. Naidu, *Kuchipudi Classical Dance* (Hyderabad: Sangeeta Nataka Akademi, 1975), pp. 25-26.
85. For a good bibliographical and biographical treatment of Jayadeva, see Patnaik, *Odissi Dance*, pp. 40-45.
86. Ibid., p. 40.
87. For the best scholarly discussion on this problem, see S.Sen, *Chandidas* (New Delhi: Sahitya Akademi, 1971), pp. 9-16.

88. For a good modern version of the Caṇḍīdāsa story and poetry, see D. Bhattacharya, *Love Songs of Chandidas* (London: George Allen & Unwin Ltd., 1967).

89. Dimock, *The Place of the Hidden Moon*, pp. 65-67.

90. Caṇḍīdāsa, quoted in D.C. Sen, *History of Bengali Language and Literature* (Calcutta: University of Calcutta, 1954), p. 45.

91. Caṇḍīdāsa, quoted in Bhattacharyya, *History of Indian Erotic Literature*, p. 90.

92. Ibid., p. 18.

93. See especially Kopf, *British Orientalism and the Bengal Renaissance*, pp. 11-42.

94. R. Schwab, *La Renaissance Orientale* (Paris: Payot, 1950).

95. J. Woodroffe, *Shakti and Shākta*, 7th ed. (Madras: Ganesh & Co., 1969), p. 407.

96. For an introduction to the process, cf. "Indian Religion as Bharata Dharma," in ibid., pp. 1-16.

97. This generation tended to support the brahmanic manner of mystifying each and every tradition, denuding them of their vital folk origins. Brahmins had been appropriating local and regional traditions for thousands of years as part of the Hindu acculturation process. In recent times, brahmins have joined modernist reform associations and have applied Western puritanical values to their own traditions.

98. For an interesting discussion of the pejorative use of "dance" in several modern Indian languages, see A. Jha, *Sexual Designs in Indian Culture* (New Delhi: Vikas Publishing House Pvt. Ltd., 1979), pp. 94-95.

99. Ibid., pp. 97-98; Vatsyayan, *Classical Indian Dance in Literature and the Arts*, pp. 161, 164.

100. What is especially interesting is the way the puritanical spirit of renaissance Hinduism has permeated the new literature on Indian dance and has been responsible for histories which make no reference to the life-style of its former practitioners. The tendency is to analyze the technical aspects of dance without any reference to its history. See, for example, Bhavnani, *The Dance in India*.

101. Sanjukta Panigrahi, the great classical Odissi dancer, has written that the dancing girls in temples of medieval Orissa "must not look at other men, must lead a chaste and celibate life, must carry out their duties with single-minded devotion," in S. Panigrahi, "A History of Dance in Orissa" (unpublished manuscript), p. 4.

102. Jha, *Sexual Designs in Indian Culture*, pp. 97-98.

103. For a good sociological discussion of why the Purāṇas took so much interest in temples as religious, social and amusement centers, see Desai, *Erotic Sculpture of India*, pp. 147-162.

104. Patnaik, *Odissi Dance*, p. 30.

105. Ibid., pp. 30-55.

106. The new de-eroticized versions of the *Gīta Govinda* in dance can be found throughout Bhavnani, *The Dance in India*.

107. See Snajukta Panigrahi's statement in note 102.

108. Patnaik, op. cit., pp. 54-56.

109. Ibid., p. 39.

110. For evidence supporting this, see ibid., pp. 41-44.

---

111. Majumdar, "Medieval Bengali Society," pp. 364-373.
112. Patnaik, op. cit., p. 43.
113. Ibid.
114 P.V. Subramaniam, "*Gita Govindam*--Piety or Plain Pornography," *Pushpanjali*, Vol. IV (November 1, 1980), p. 107.

Bibliography

Agnihotri, V., *Fallen Women* (Kanpur: Maharaja, n.d.).

Bernier, F., *Travels in the Mogul Empire*, translated by A. Constable (Oxford: Oxford University Press, 1934).

Bhattacharya, D., *Love Songs of Chandidas* (London: George Allen & Unwin Ltd., 1967).

Bhattacharyya, N.N., *History of Indian Erotic Literature* (New Delhi: Munshiram Manoharlal Publishers Pvt. Ltd., 1975).

Bhattacharyya, N.N., *History of the Tantric Religion* (New Delhi: Manohar, 1982).

Bhattacharyya, N.N., *The Indian Mother Goddess* (New Delhi: Manohar, 1977).

Bhavnani, E., *The Dance in India* (Bombay: D.B. Taraporevala Sons & Co. Private Ltd., 1979).

Boulding, E., *The Underside of History* (Boulder, Colorado: Westview Press, 1976).

Briffault, R., *The Mothers* (New York: Macmillan Company, 1927).

Bullough, V. and B. Bullough, *An Illustrated Social History of Prostitution* (New York: Crown Publishers, Inc., 1978).

De, S.K., *Ancient Indian Erotics and Erotic Literature* (Calcutta: Firma K.L. Mukhopadhyay, 1959).

Desai, D., *Erotic Sculpture of India: A Socio-Cultural Study* (New Delhi: Tata McGraw-Hill Publishing Co., 1975).

Dimock, E.C., *The Place of the Hidden Moon* (Chicago, Illinois: University of Chicago Press, 1966).

Dubois, Abbe J.A., *Hindu Manners, Customs and Ceremonies*, translated by H.K. Beauchamp (Oxford: Clarendon Press, 1906).

Eliade, M., *Yoga: Immortality and Freedom*, tranlated by W.R. Trask (New York: Pantheon Books, 1958).

Ellis, H., *The Dance of Life* (New York: Modern Library, 1929).

Forbes, G., "Inside Pushing Back the Walls: A Study of the Indian Women's Movement." (Unpublished manuscript.)

Friedrich, P., *The Meaning of Aphrodite* (Chicago, Illinois: University of Chicago Press, 1978).

Guenther, H.V., *The Tantric View of Life* (London: Shambhala, 1976).

Guenther, H.V., *Yuganaddha: The Tantric View of Life* (Varanasi: Chowkhamba Sanskrit Series, 1952).

Hall, N., *The Moon and the Virgin* (New York: Harper & Row, 1980).

Harding, M.E., *Woman's Mysteries, Ancient and Modern* (New York: Harper and Row, 1976).

Jha, A., *Sexual Designs in Indian Culture* (New Delhi: Vikas Publishing House Pvt. Ltd., 1979).

Kakati, B.K., *The Mother Goddess Kāmākhyā* (Gauhati, Assam: K.C. Pal, 1967).

Kopf, D., *British Orientalism and the Bengal Renaissance* (Berkeley, California: University of California Press, 1969).

Lal, K., *Apsaras of Khajurāho* (Delhi: Asia Press, 1966).

Lal, K., *The Cult of Desire* (Delhi: Asia Press, 1966).

Lal, K., *The Religion of Love* (Delhi: Arts & Letters, 1971).

Macmunn, Sir G., *The Religions and Hidden Cults of India* (Delhi: Oriental Publishers, 1975).

Majumdar, R.C., "Medieval Bengali Society," in R.C. Majumdar, ed., *The History of Bengal: Hindu Period* (Dacca: University of Dacca, 1943).

Marglin, F.A., *Wives of the God-King: The Rituals of the Devadasis of Puri* (Delhi: Oxford University Press, 1985).

Monier-Williams, M., *Hinduism* (London: Society for Promoting Christian Knowledge, 1925).

Naidu, M.A., *Kuchipudi Classical Dance* (Hyderabad: Sangeeta Nataka Akademi, 1975).

Panigrahi, S., "A History of Dance in Orissa." (Unpublished manuscript.)

Patnaik, D.N., *Odissi Dance* (Bhubaneswar: Orissa Sangeet Natak Akademi, 1971).

Payne, E.A., *The Śāktas* (Oxford: Oxford University Press, 1933).

Punekar, S.D., *A Study of Prostitutes in Bombay* (Bombay: Lalvani Publishing House, 1967).

Rao, M.R., *The Prostitutes of Hyderabad* (Hyderabad: Association for Moral and Social Hygiene in India, n.d.).

Sattar, A., *In the Sylvan Shadows* (Dacca: Saquib Brothers, 1971).

Schwab, R., *La Renaissance Orientale* (Paris: Payot, 1950).

Sen, D.C., *History of Bengali Language and Literature* (Calcutta: University of Calcutta, 1954).

Sen, S., *Chandidas* (New Delhi: Sahitya Akademi, 1971).

Spink, W., *The Axis of Eros* (New York: Penguin Books, 1973).

Stone, M., *When God Was A Woman* (New York: Harcourt, Brace, Jovanovich, 1978).

Subramaniam, P.V., "*Gita Govindam*--Piety or Plain Pornography," *Pushpanjali*, Vol. IV (November 1, 1980).

Travedi, H.R., *Scheduled Caste Women: Studies in Exploitation* (Delhi: Concept Publishing Company, 1977).

Van Buitenen, J.A.B., *Two Plays of Ancient India* (New York: Columbia University Press, 1968).

Vatsyayan, K., *Classical Indian Dance in Literature and the Arts* (New Delhi: Sangeet Natak Akademi, 1968).

Vatsyayana, *Kāma Sūtra*, translated by S.C. Upadhyaya (Bombay: Taraporevala Sons & Co., 1970).

Watts, A., *Erotic Spirituality* (New York: Macmillan Company, 1971).

Woodroffe, J., *Shakti and Shākta*, 7th ed. (Madras: Ganesh & Co., 1969).

Glossary

abhaya mudrā: hand gesture of palm facing outward, signifying "do not fear" (see Chapter V, Plate 10).

abhinaya: ways or means of expressing, evoking or suggesting emotions; ways in which a dancer interprets a poetic text; the four kinds of *abhinaya* traditionally recognized as aspects of drama and dance are: (1) *āṅgika abhinaya*, gestures of the body or any of its parts; (2) *vācika abhinaya*, speech and song; (3) *sāttvika abhinaya*, imitation of involuntary expressions of emotional states, such as trembling, weeping, etc.; in the context of Bharata Nāṭyam, *sāttvika abhinaya* also refers to imbuing the performance with soul, life, feeling, and subtlety, evocative of *rasa*; and (4) *āhārya abhinaya*, dress and make-up.

abhinaya hasta: hand gesture employed in mimetic/expressive dance (see Colorplates V-VIII).

aḍavu: basic unit of pure or abstract dance (see Chapter III, Figures 1-3, 5-11).

ādi tāla: metrical cycle of 4+2+2 pulses.

Advaita Vedānta: non-dualistic school of philosophy regarded as the end or fulfillment of the Vedas; its most illustrious exponent was Śaṅkara (8th cent. A.D.).

Āgamas: a class of sacred texts containing prescriptions for modes of temple worship.

alaṃkāra: ornament; figure of speech; figurative language.

alaṃkāradāsī: female dancer performing at family functions, such as weddings.

alaṃkāra śāstra: poetics; rhetoric; aesthetics.

alapadma hasta: single-hand gesture (see Chapter III, Figure 4c).

ālāpana: a free, non-metric improvisation which brings out the essential characteristics of the *rāga* proper, to which it serves as an introduction.

alārippu: opening item in a Bharata Nāṭyam recital: a pure dance piece which is an invocation addressed to the gods and the audience.

alaukika: extraordinary or transcendental experience.

Āḻvārs: Tamil Vaiṣṇavite *bhakti* saints.

amṛta: nectar of immortality.

ānanda: supreme bliss.

ānanda tāṇḍava: dance of bliss, associated with Śiva's dance of destruction and liberation, represented most frequently in the typical iconic pose of Śiva as Naṭarāja, or The Lord of Dance (see Chapter V, Plates 3 & 10).

aṅgahāra: an extended sequence of dance movements composed of constituent movements known as *karaṇas* and *mātṛkās*.

aṅgas: major limbs, such as head, neck, hands, etc., classified for purposes of mimetic/expressive dance.

añjali mudrā: gesture of reverence with palms joined as in prayer.

anubhāva: "consequent," overt expression of an emotional state.

anupallavi: a section of a musical compostion which emphasizes the lower melodic range, and usually follows as a melodic contrast to another section of the composition known as *pallavi*.

apsaras: celestial nymph or dancing girl of the gods.

asaṃyuta hasta: gesture of single hand, e.g., *alapadma*, *tripatāka*, *haṃsāsya* (see Chapter III, Figure 4).

ātodya: instrumental music.

bhakti: intense religious devotion to the deity of one's choice.

bhāva: emotion.

bhoga: enjoyment.

Bhujaṅgāñcita: "Serpent Touch," *karaṇa* no. 40.

Bhujaṅgatrāsita: "Frightened by a Serpent," *karaṇa* no. 24 (see Chapter V, Plate 5).

Bhujaṅgatrasta Recita: "Reeling with Serpent Fright," *karaṇa* no. 35.

Brahman: Ultimate Reality in the Upaniṣads (the concluding portions of the Vedas) and in the schools Vedānta philosophy based upon them.

caraṇa: third section of a larger musical composition, using melodic variants of the preceding *pallavi* and *anupallavi* as well as new melodic material.

cārī: gait (in dance).
chanda: a metric unit of verse.
citrasūtram: canon of painting.

darpaṇa: mirror.
darśana: vision of God.
deśī: popular or folk drama, dance, or music.
devadāsī: literally, female servant of god--female temple dancer.
dhvani: "resonance," suggestion in poetry--a term coined by Ānandavardhana (9th cent. A.D.).
dola hasta: "swing" gesture, the arm slung low (see Colorplate III and Chapter V, Plates 1&9).
dola pāda: a swinging gait, such as that of an elephant (see Chapter V, Plate 12).
Durgā Mahiṣāsuramardinī: Durgā slaying the Buffalo-demon.
dūta: male messenger.
dūtī: female messenger.

gadya: prose.
gaja hasta: arm thrown across the chest, elephant trunk-like (see Chapter V, Plate 3).
Gajakrīḍita: "Playing Like an Elephant," *karaṇa* no. 68 (see Chapter V, Plate 12).
gamaka: ornament--commonly used to refer to embellishment in music.
gaṇas: Śiva's troop of dwarfs, usually portrayed as devilishly comic characters.
Gaṇeśa: "Lord of *gaṇas*," elephant-headed god, regarded as remover of obstacles, son of Śiva and Pārvatī.
gīta: vocal music.
gopī: cowherdess, milkmaid.
gopuram: South Indian temple gateway surmounted by soaring tower.
guru: teacher, mentor, spiritual preceptor.
guru-śiṣya paramparā: teacher-to-pupil line of transmission.

haṃsāsya hasta: single-hand gesture (see Chapter III, Figure 4b).
Harijan: "child of god," epithet of the untouchable, coined by Gandhi.
hasta mudrā: hand gesture.
hāvas: amorous gestures, spontaneous or deliberate; examples of spontaneous amorous gestures are: (manifestations of) *vilāsa*, delight; *vibhrama*, confusion; *kilakiñcita*, hysteria; examples of deliberate amorous gestures are: *līlā*, playfulness; *lalita*, lolling in a graceful pose; *kuṭṭamita*, pretending anger; *bibboka*, affecting indifference.
Huduma: a fertility ritual of Rajbansis (a tribe of East Bengal).

Ita Pūjā: dance ritual of Rajbansis to bring forth rain.

Jagannātha: "Lord of the World," epithet of Viṣṇu.
jaṭās: gyrating "dread locks" of Śiva Naṭarāja (Śiva as The Lord of Dance).
jati: complex rhythmic pattern consisting of a sequence of *aḍavus* or basic units of pure dance movements, executed to the recitation of *sollukaṭṭu* (rhythmic syllables) by the *naṭṭuvanar*.
jatisvaram: a rhythmically complex pure dance item.
jāvali: a light, romantic, expressive dance item whose typical theme is worldly love.
jīvātma: individual soul.
jogti: whore.

kalāpaka: three *karaṇas* combined.
Kāma: Indian god of love.
karaṇa: a basic movement of dance, involving the coordination of hands and feet, described in the *Nāṭyaśāstra* (see Chapter V, Plates 7,8).
kaṭakāmukha hasta: "opening in a link," single-hand gesture (See Colorplate III).
Kathak: North Indian classical dance.
Kathākali a type of dance drama of Kerala.
Khamās: a *rāga* evocative of *śṛṅgāra rasa* (erotic love).
korvai: A coherent sequence of *aḍavus*.

kriyā: activity.

Kucipuḍi: dance of Andhra Pradesh.

kula deva: patron deity, as of a royal dynasty.

kumārī: virgin; girl; daughter.

Kuravañji: a type of dance drama of Tamil Nadu.

lāsya: lyrical, graceful, feminine style of dancing.

latā hasta: "hanging like a vine," single-hand gesture (see Chapter V, Plate 12).

laukika: ordinary, worldly--as contrasted with *alaukika*, or extraordinary, transcendent; regarded as characterizing ordinary experience as distinguished from aesthetic experience.

līlā: play; the universe and the flow of events regarded as the sporting recreation of the creator god.

liṅgam: phallus--most commonly worshipped emblem of Śiva.

lokadharmī: realistic or naturalistic style of dramatic performance or mimetic dance.

māhārī: Oriya (language of Orissa) term for a *devadāsī*.

maithuna: sexual intercourse.

Maṇipurī: classical dance of Manipur.

mārgī: classical, as contrasted with popular or folk--whether in music, dance, or drama.

mātṛkā: two *karaṇas* combined.

māyā: magic; the phenomenal world as illusion.

mēḷa: a "parent" pitch-set of a *rāga*.

Mohiniāṭṭam: dance of Kerala

mokṣa: liberation or final release from the cycle of rebirths.

mṛdaṅgam: a double-headed barrel-shaped drum of South India.

mṛdaṅgam tani: a solo section or composition for *mṛdaṅgam*.

mudrā: "sign" or gesture.

muktāyi svara: a pre-composed section of pitches sung as solfege and then with text; sung between the *anupallavi* and *caraṇa* sections of a *varṇam* composition.

Murugan: Tamil god of beauty, fertility, and war; considered identical with Skanda, the son of Śiva.

Naṭarāja (or *Naṭeśa*): "The Lord of Dance," epithet of Śiva.

naṭṭu aḍavu: A type of basic unit of pure dance movement together with its variants, known as an *aḍavu* group (see Chapter III, Figures 3, 5-11).

naṭṭuvanar: dance master; musical accompanist of dancer(s).

nāṭya: drama; in the context of dance, elements of plot and drama (see Colorplates VI-VIII).

nāṭyadharmī: conventional or stylized manner of dramatic performance or mimetic dance.

Nāṭyaśālā: dance hall or theater.

nāyaka: male protagonist, or hero.

Nāyaṉārs: Tamil Śaivite *bhakti* saints.

nāyikā: female protagonist, or heroine; the *Nāṭyaśāstra* enumerates eight types of *nāyikās,* according to their situation, as follows:
(1) *vāsakasajjā*, "one dressed up for union [with her lover]";
(2) *virahotkaṇṭhitā*, "one distressed by separation";
(3) *svādhīnabhartṛkā*, "one having her husband in subjection";
(4) *kalahāntaritā*, "one separated from her lover by a quarrel";
(5) *khaṇḍitā*, "one enraged with her lover";
(6) *vipralabdhā*, "one deceived by her lover";
(7) *proṣitabhartṛkā,* "one whose husband has gone on a journey"; and
(8) *abhisārikā*, "one who goes [to her lover]."

neti-neti: "not this-not this"--categorical denial of the ultimate reality of anything but Brahman, the non-qualified One.

Nirvāṇa: a state in which all craving has been extinguished ("blown out"), positively characterized as wisdom and bliss; the ultimate goal of spiritual discipline in Buddhism; in some contexts viewed negatively as other than and beyond the flux of phenomena.

nṛtta: pure dance (see Frontispiece and Colorplates I-IV).

nṛtta hasta: hand gesture employed in pure (non-mimetic) dance (see Frontispiece and Colorplates I-IV).

nṛtta śāstra: canon of dance.

nṛtya: mimetic or expressive dance; term used synonymously with *abhinaya* (see Colorplates V-VIII).

Odissi: classical dance of Orissa.

padam: a leisurely interpretive dance item expressive of the heroine's love for a god.
padmakośa hasta: single-hand gesture employed in mimetic dance (see Colorplate V).
padya: verse.
pallavi: a section of a musical composition which consists of three movements, i.e., *pallavi, anupallavi* and *caraṇa*.
Paramātma: the soul of the universe.
patāka hasta: single-hand gesture employed both in pure and mimetic dance (see Colorplate I).
pīṭha: a shrine of the Goddess (Śiva's spouse).
prabhāvalī: "arc of glory," large halo around an image (see Chapter V, Plate 3).
Prakṛti: Nature, primal matter.
pratimā lakṣaṇam: canon of image-making.
pratyaṅgas: minor limbs, such as shoulders, arms, back, thighs, etc., classified for purposes of mimetic/expressive dance.
prema: spiritual love, or love of God.
pūjā: worship.
Punnāgavarāḷi: a *rāga* evocative of *karuṇa rasa* (compassion).
Purāṇas: "stories of old," sacred texts, compendia of Hindu myths and religous instruction.
Puruṣa: Spirit.

rāga: a melodic mode distinguished by pitch selection and hierarchy, ascent/descent, scale pattern, etc.
rāgamālikā: "garland of *rāgas*," a composition for a dance item, consisting of a series of *rāgas*.
rājadāsī: female dancer performing at a royal court.
rasa: aesthetic mood.
rasāsvāda: aesthetic delectation, savoring a work of art.

rasika: one capable of tasting *rasa*; term used interchangeably with *sahṛdaya*.

recita: arms thrown upwards.

ṛṣi: seer, sage.

śabdam: typical first *abhinaya* (mimetic/expressive) item in a Bharata Nāṭyam recital, executed to a song in praise of a god or royal patron.

sādhu: holy man; monk.

Śahāna: a *rāga* evocative of *karuṇa rasa* (compassion).

sāhitya: poetic or literary text interpreted by vocalist and dancer.

sahṛdaya: "like-hearted one," one capable of aesthetic response; term used interchangeably with *rasika*.

sakhī: heroine's female companion, confidante and go-between.

Śakti cult: cult of the Goddess as creative energy of the universe.

śālabhañjikā: female tree spirit (see Frontispiece).

saṃghātaka: five *karaṇas* combined.

saṃkathā: conversation.

Sampradāya: a teacher-student descent group within a dance form such as Bharata Nāṭyam.

saṃyuta hasta: gesture of both hands combined, e.g., *puṣpapuṭa* (see Chapter V, Plate 11).

sañcāri bhāvas: see *vyabhicāri bhāvas*.

śaṇḍaka: four *karaṇas* combined.

śāstra: treatise; field of knowledge; science.

sāttvika alaṃkāras: natural graces of women; e.g., *śobhā*, beauty; *kānti*, loveliness; *dīpti*, radiance; *mādhurya*, sweetness.

sāttvika bhāvas: involuntary manifestations of emotional states, such as blushing, trembling, weeping, etc.

śilpa: the visual arts; sculpture.

siṃhakarṇa mudrā: "lion's ears," a hand gesture with little index finger slightly crimped; the *hasta* or *mudrā* by which the Goddess holds a lotus blossom (see Chapter V, Plates 1&9).

Śivakāmasundarī: "Śiva's Beloved Beauty," epithet of Śiva's spouse Pārvatī.

śloka: a short religious verse; an optional expressive dance piece devotional in nature, used as an opening or closing of a Bharata Nāṭyam performance.

sollukaṭṭu: mnemonic syllables recited in rhythmic phrases, representing strokes on the drum or dance movements.

śṛṅgāra bhakti (or *madhura bhakti*): passionate love of God.

śṛṅgāra rasa: the aesthetic mood of erotic love; *śṛṅgāra* is the dominant *rasa* in much of Indian traditional poetry, drama, literature, and the arts. Two states of *śṛṅgāra* are *vipralambha*, love in separation, and *saṃbhoga*, love in enjoyment. Ten stages of love in separation or unfulfilled love are traditionally recognized: (1) *ābhilāsa*, longing; (2) *cintā*, anxiety; (3) *anusmṛti*, recollection; (4) *guṇakīrtana*, enumeration of (the beloved's) merits; (5) *udvega*, distress; (6) *vilāpa*, lamentation; (7) *unmāda*, insanity; (8) *vyādhi*, sickness; (9) *jaḍatā*, stupor; (10) *maraṇa*, death.

śruti box: drone instrument.

sthānaka: dance position.

sthāyi bhāvas: stable or dominant emotions; nine *sthāyi bhāvas* and their corresponding *rasas* are traditionally recognized; they are as follows:

Sthāyi Bhāva	***Rasa***
rati: sexual passion	*śṛṅgāra*; erotic love
hāsa: laughter	*hāsya*: humor
śoka: sorrow	*karuṇa*: compassion
krodha: anger	*raudra*: fury
utsāha: fortitude	*vīra*: heroism
bhaya: fear	*bhayānaka*: terror
jugupsā: disgust	*bībhatsa*: loathing
vismaya: astonishment	*adbhuta*: wonder
śama: equanimity	*śānta*: tranquility

sūtradhāra: stage manager or director of a play.

svaras: notes; mnemonic syllables (solfege type) representing musical pitches: Sa, Ri, Ga, Ma, Pa, Da, Ni, Sa.

svarajati: centerpiece of a Bharata Nāṭyam program, alternative to *varṇam*.

tala: a rhythmic structure; a metrical cycle made up of one or more subdivisions; e.g., *ādi tāla*: 4+2+2 pulses.

tāḷam: small bronze cymbals played by the dance master. (*naṭṭuvanar*), used to render the rhythmic beats which guide the footwork of the dancer.

Talapuṣpapuṭa: "Palms Cupped with Flowers," *karaṇa* no. 1 (see Chapter V, Plate 11).

tāṇḍava: forceful, masculine style of dancing.

tānpura: drone instrument (stringed).

Tantrism: a spiritual discipline which, in its Hindu variety, is predominantly centered on the worship of Śakti, the Goddess as creative energy of the universe, and involves elaborate rituals rich in symbolism, as well as a special kind of meditative practice known as Kuṇḍalinī yoga, for the purpose of attaining spiritual emancipation or worldly power.

tatti mettu: rhythmic stamping of feet in pure dance; an *aḍavu* group (cf. *naṭṭu aḍavu*).

taṭṭu aḍavu: an *aḍavu* group (cf. *naṭṭu aḍavu*; see Chapter III, Figures 1-3).

tillāna: concluding item in a Bharata Nāṭyam program--a pure dance piece, featuring dazzling footwork and sculpturesque poses.

tirmānam: a sequence of dance movements in the form of rhythmic flourishes, executed to the recitation of *sollukaṭṭu* (rhythmic syllables) by the *naṭṭuvanar*.

tiruvāci: fiery nimbus of flames around Naṭarāja and other images (see Chapter V, Plate 3).

tribhaṅga: three-bend body pose characteristic of Indian sculpture and Odissi dance (see Chapter V, Plates 1&9).

Tripatāka hasta: single-hand gesture (see Chapter III, Figure 4a).

upāṅgas: facial features, such as eyes, nose, cheeks, lips, etc., classified for purposes of mimetic/expressive dance.

ūrdhva tāṇḍava: a form of dance of Śiva.

Vaiṣṇava Sahajiyā: a Bengali sect of Vaiṣṇavism.

varṇam (or *pada varṇam*): centerpiece of a Bharata Nāṭyam program--a highly complex dance number in which pure and mimetic/expressive dance alternate.

Veṅkateśvara: a form of Viṣṇu.

vibhāva: "determinant," observable cause of emotional state.

vimāna: temple sanctuary.

vīṇā: South Indian stringed instrument.

viniyoga: usage or range of meanings of a gesture or movement in mimetic dance.

Viṣṇukrānta: "Viṣṇu's Stride," *karaṇa* no. 100 (see Chapter V, Plate 6).

vyabhicāri bhāvas (also *sañcāri bhāvas*): transitory or subsidiary emotional states.

yakṣa (male), *yakṣī* (female): a semi-divine being associated with wealth, fertility of the earth, and vegetation.

Yakṣagāna: a type of dance drama of Karnataka.

yoginīs: a class of nuns leading austere lives of prayer and meditation.